SEWING FREEDOM

SEWING FREEDOM:
PHILIP JOSEPHS, TRANSNATIONALISM
& EARLY NEW ZEALAND ANARCHISM

Jared Davidson

AK
PRESS
EDINBURGH · OAKLAND · BALTIMORE

Sewing Freedom: Philip Josephs, Transnationalism & Early New Zealand Anarchism
© 2013 Jared Davidson. This edition © 2013 AK Press (Oakland, Edinburgh, Baltimore)

ISBN: 978-1-84935-132-4 | eBook ISBN: 978-1-84935-133-1
Library of Congress Control Number: 2013930243

AK Press	AK Press
674-A 23rd Street	PO Box 12766
Oakland, CA 94612	Edinburgh EH8 9YE
USA	Scotland
www.akpress.org	www.akuk.com
akpress@akpress.org	ak@akedin.demon.co.uk

The above addresses would be delighted to provide you with the latest AK Press distribution
catalog, which features the several thousand books, pamphlets, zines, audio and video products,
and stylish apparel published and/or distributed by AK Press. Alternatively, visit our websites
for the complete catalog, latest news, and secure ordering.

Visit us at:
www.akpress.org
www.akuk.com
www.revolutionbythebook.akpress.org

Set in Dante and Officina San ITC Black.
Cover and Interior design by Jared Davidson.
Illustrations by Alec Icky Dunn.
Printed in the United States on acid-free, recycled paper.

In memory of Edna Davidson

CONTENTS

Acknowledgements 9

Foreword by Barry Pateman 11

Introduction 17

1 Rising expectations and dashed hopes 23

2 Glasgow and the anarchists 29

3 A workingman's paradise? 39

4 Wellington's working-class counter-culture 51

5 To hell with law and authority 65

6 An agent of freedom 103

7 No war but class war 113

8 Parasites, anarchists, and other IWW types 125

9 Loose ends 135

Epilogue 143

APPENDICES

Trades unionism in New Zealand: Is it a faliure? 149

The general strike as a weapon against conscription 152

List of books and papers found in Philip Josephs' possession 155

Endnotes 159

Illustration sources 174

ACKNOWLEDGEMENTS

This research would not have been possible without the advice and support of many others whose names do not grace the cover. Early work on the New Zealand far left (and their adversaries) by Bert Roth, Frank Prebble, Kerry Taylor, Eric Olssen, Mark Derby, and Richard Hill paved the way for this book. Kerry and Mark were always forthcoming with obscure bits of information, Barry Pateman sent me numerous goodies from his American and British vaults (as well as penning the thoughtful foreword), Peter Clayworth raced down to Archives New Zealand for some last-minute additions, and Urs Signer translated a rare find from German. They also took the time to look over the final manuscript, as did Caroline Josephs, Richard Hill, Ryan Bodman, Lucien van der Walt, Philip Wills, Sophie Taptiklis, David Berry, and Stuart Moriarty-Patten. A hearty thank you for your help, insights, and suggestions. Stuart's request to look over his 2012 thesis on the New Zealand IWW was fortuitous—it is easily the most comprehensive study of the New Zealand Wobblies to date, and discussion with Stuart around our respective work was both stimulating and clarifying.

I especially want to acknowledge the relatives of Philip and Sophia, who embraced me and the project with open arms—and even bought me lunch. Caroline Josephs, Naomi Gillmore, Helen Dukes, Stacey Dukes, Philip Bourke, Joe Stanley, Ivy Raff, Sue Hillman, Jessica Cook, Lindon Richards, and Carol Baillie provided valuable information on the lives of their extraordinary ancestors or helped me to find long-lost cousins. It was amazing to meet some of you in person, and I sincerely hope this work serves the family well.

We have Jesse Meek, Mark Derby, and Lorna to thank for the proof reading, Alec Icky Dunn for the excellent illustrations, and all of the crew at AK Press for supporting this project in every way possible.

Particular thanks are due to the Institute for Anarchist Studies, whose grant enabled me to employ the studious Teun van Lier to unearth large amounts of information at the International Institute of Social History in Amsterdam (IISH)—something I could never have afforded myself. Staff at the IISH, Kate Sharpley Library, Labadie Collection, Scottish Jewish Archives Centre, Archives New Zealand, Alexander Turnbull Library, National Library of New Zealand, Hocken Library, Macmillan Brown Library, JC Beaglehole Room, Canterbury Museum, Crown Law Office, New Zealand Jewish Archives, University of Leicester, and the University of Stirling have helped me considerably, especially due to the fact that offshore travel was not an option.

I'd also like to thank Philip Ruff, Julie Herrada, Nicholas Evans, Terri Marquez, Mairtin Sean O'Cathain, Hershl Hartman, Alex Frame, Harvey Kaplan, Constance Bantman, Kate Hutchens, Melanie Nolan, Verity Burgmann, James Bennett, Kenneth Collins, William Kenefick, Steven Fraser, Lorna Wuthrich, Lorraine Martin, Lynley Short, Stevan Eldred-Grigg, Peter Franks, Mark Crookston, Thomasin Sleigh, Mark Goodman, Cathy Marr, Stefanie Lash, Anna Blackman, Erin Kimber, Sue Hirst, Dave Welch, David Combs, Josh Macphee, Julie Robins, Michael Sibir, Marilyn and the many Roots Chat members, Allison Page, Antra Celmins, Maria Katsikandarakis, Anthony Einfeld, David Einfeld, Heidi Kuglin, Helen Tulett, Charles Eigl, Beyond Resistance, and Katipo Books (apologies to anyone I have missed). Whether it was email advice, archive requests, or putting me up in Wellington for a night, the above were all willing to help.

Finally, I want to say a huge thank you to Zoe and Meredith, the crew at Cardijn House and my extended family, who offered me love and support throughout this research, despite enduring absences, endless rhetoric, and outbursts of excitement. The fact that this book exists is testament to their patience, especially considering that my writing is an after-work activity. With that in mind, I would like to add that any mistakes herein are my own.

Jared Davidson
February 2013

FOREWORD BY BARRY PATEMAN

This is a fine book that sheds another clear beam of light on the complex puzzle that is anarchist history. Meticulously researched, sometimes following barely perceivable trails, thoughtful and incisive, it presents us with an as yet uncharted anarchist history in a controlled and engaging way. Like all good history, it leaves us with much to think about; and, like all good anarchist history, it encourages us to consider how we read, interrogate, and assess the long and sometimes confusing journey towards anarchy.

Individuals and their actions are the fuses running through our movement and it is right that we recognize Philip Josephs as part of this tradition. His journey from Latvia to New Zealand was long, arduous, and—one senses—educational. Somewhere along the journey the experiences of his life, the influences of his milieu, and his own emotional make up led him to anarchism. That in itself is a marvellous story and needs to be discovered and told, not only about Josephs but about so many other comrades as well. Josephs' remarkable journey led him to play a seminal role in how anarchism developed in New Zealand.

That there was anarchist practice in New Zealand before the arrival of Josephs is made clear by the author. Anarchist contributions to pubic debates, strike actions, and suggestions of influence from exiled comrades were all part of this milieu. Some obviously identified with some sense of 'anarchist' and carried that influence within their communities. By working with the most prolific English-language publishers of his day (Freedom Press in London and the Mother Earth Publishing Association in New York), Josephs organized a regular flow of current anarchist-communist propaganda into Wellington. All this helped to build a working class, oppositional counter-culture in New Zealand, one that proved to be persistently resilient.

We are reminded again by Josephs' experience of the role of the bookshop in the history of, and developments within, anarchism. Bookshops such as Charlie Lahr's in London during the 1920s and 30s and William McDevitt's in San Francisco in the early part of the twentieth century played similar roles as Josephs' store did (if they were, at times, a tad more literary!). They provided a place where people could engage with written and spoken ideas; ideas that clashed, contradicted, or complimented each other, but ideas nevertheless. Some of these ideas were new, some simply re-enforcing previously held feelings and thoughts, some were confusing and never fully understood, and some apparently irrelevant. These stores provided a physical place for people to meet, to argue, to think, and to make friends and enemies. Ideas left the safety and confines of their author's head and became tested and refined by the experience of the world at large. We can find these places in every town and every city where anarchism began to grow, full of newspapers, pamphlets, books, scraps of paper advertising meetings and above all, possibilities. Bookstores were a link to a wider world, a community of which you were a member. Besides pamphlets and books, Josephs' shop stocked papers such as *The Herald of Revolt* from Glasgow and *The Agitator* from Home Colony, Washington State, US. Beyond your neighbourhood, beyond New Zealand, there were others thinking like you and offering support and solidarity. You and your friends were not alone.

This book reminds us of those tiresome but still critical questions that reverberate across the years, questions that need to be addressed even now. Who can and should anarchists work with as they mount their attacks on capitalism? What tactics should we use, and how malleable and flexible can they be, yet still remain anarchist? How can anarchists adapt to the national situation they find themselves in, while still remaining internationalists in outlook and practice? Above all, what is it that makes people anarchists and not syndicalists, or libertarian communists, or individualists, or whatever? Make no mistake—they saw a difference and the very least we can do is to explore it. To ignore their self-perception leads to the danger of building a reductive and one-dimensional view of history. These complexities and differences are ignored at cost to us and with some arrogance to them.

Josephs' life gives us pause to reflect on an equally critical matter. As we have already mentioned, it was Josephs who brought so much current anarchist propaganda to New Zealand. It is hard to judge what was already available, but probably very little. We do know that some people had moved organically towards some definition of anarchism. What Josephs did was bring accepted written anarchism to New Zealand—Kropotkin, Goldman et al set the parameters of anarchist communism and, perhaps, formalized what people had been thinking and doing for all those years. Just how people move to anarchist ideas without the help of these writings continues to be a rich area for research and discussion. Some concentrated understanding of how people framed the written word would also bear fruitful examination. All those pamphlets folded and put in a pocket to read at work, at home, in the pub, or on the bus. Did they simply re-enforce what these people already felt—that marvellous shock of recognition when your feelings and thoughts are validated by the written word? Did they confuse the reader? Did they make them too self-critical or puzzled? We need to ask how these readers processed what they had read in the light of their own experiences. They were not empty vessels waiting to be filled by the word. A dialogue of sorts took place between each one of their ideas and experiences and the written idea. Finding that dialogue and tracing how it developed just might lead us to consider how anarchist ideas and practice progressed. The published word aimed at a public audience can only take us so far, and the very last thing we should do is mistake it for a finished history. Anarchists often make themselves rather than being made.

New Zealand has a rich history of anarchism and a rich present of practice. Some comrades have recently shown exemplary courage and resilience when faced by the might of the state. Many are working tirelessly in their communities, taking on the countless repressions and cruelties that make up the personality and practice of capitalism. Such courage and resilience echoes that shown by Josephs and his comrades all those years ago. We are extremely lucky to have Jared Davidson to remind us of it.

"To us in New Zealand Anarchism seems a far-away peril. That is an illusion. Wherever there is private property and any sort of Government, there may appear the Anarchist."

Otago Witness, 27 November 1901

INTRODUCTION

Philip Josephs—a Latvian-born Jewish tailor, recent arrival to New Zealand by way of Scotland, and self-proclaimed anarchist—took to the floor of the 1906 Wellington May Day demonstration amidst orchestral outbursts and a flurry of motions. "This meeting," moved Josephs, "sends its fraternal greetings to our comrades engaged in the universal class war, and pledges itself to work for the abolition of the capitalistic system and the substitution in New Zealand of a co-operative commonwealth, founded on the collective ownership of the land and the means of production and distribution."[1] The motion, as well as highlighting his involvement in the radical milieu of New Zealand's capital, conveys the key concepts of his anarchism: internationalism, class struggle, and free communism.

However, if readers were to form an understanding of anarchism based on the newspapers of the day or from the accounts of New Zealand's labour movement by certain historians, a very different conclusion would be drawn. On the occasions it is mentioned, anarchism is used hysterically by the press to denounce or decry; by labour leaders in order to show the fallacy of their opponents' positions; and by Labourist historians to symbolise wayward ideas or acts of extremism—painting a nightmarish picture of anarchist practice in the vein of Chesterton's *The Man Who Was Thursday*.[2]

Unfortunately, this is not a trend restricted to New Zealand. Anarchism as a philosophy and a movement has long been misrepresented,as French anarchist Daniel Guérin notes:

> Those who would slander anarchism serve up a tendentious interpretation of its doctrine. Anarchism is essentially individualistic, particularistic, hostile to any form of organization. It leads to

fragmentation, to the egocentric withdrawal to small local units of administration and production. It is incapable of centralizing or of planning. It is nostalgic for the 'golden age.' It tends to resurrect archaic social forms. It suffers from childish optimism; its 'idealism' takes no account of the solid realities of the material infrastructure. It is incurably petit-bourgeois; it places itself outside of the class movement of the modern proletariat... and finally, certain commentators take care to rescue from oblivion and to draw attention only to its most controversial deviations, such as terrorism, individual assassinations, propaganda by explosives.[3]

Yet as Vadim Damier illustrates, anarchism was a global working class movement, one "that spread to countries as different as Spain and Russia, France and Japan, Argentina and Sweden, Italy and China, Portugal and Germany," and "was able to attract hundreds of thousands, indeed millions, of wage workers." Anarchists "not only took an active part in the most important social upheavals and conflicts of the twentieth century, often leaving their own indelible imprint on these events, but also in many countries they formed the centre of a special, inimitable, working class culture with its own values, norms, customs, and symbols."[4] Against this reality of anarchism as a socialist movement, a focus on 'its most controversial deviations' reaffirms the stereotype of the anarchist terrorist, dressed in black and wielding a bomb—dangerous, malcontent, and against civilisation itself. "'God's Own Country' is not safe from the vagaries of the person who believes in the bomb as opposed to argument," bellowed one New Zealand daily paper in 1907.[5]

Although highly exaggerated, this newspaper article contained one truth: God's Own Country—the 'Workingman's Paradise' that was New Zealand in the early years of the twentieth century—had anarchists in its midst. To describe them as a coherently organized movement would be another exaggeration, but nonetheless, those that subscribed to anarchism in New Zealand were a valid part of the wider labour movement, imparting uncredited ideas, tactics, and influence. Likewise, anarchist agitation and the circulation of radical literature contributed significantly to the development of a radical working-class counterculture in New Zealand.

Yet unfortunately, these radicals have fared badly in labour historiography—even more so than their communist counterparts who, at least, are mentioned, even if they are "frequently dealt with by a very brief, generally dismissive, characterisation, often little more than a caricature."[6] New Zealand anarchists and their commitment to social change deserve more than the relative silence that currently represents their struggle.

Indeed, the most substantial work to date on anarchism in New Zealand during the twentieth century's turbulent teens is the indispensable thirty-two-page pamphlet, "'Troublemakers' Anarchism and Syndicalism: The Early Years of the Libertarian Movement in Aotearoa/New Zealand," by Frank Prebble. Drawing on snippets of primary and secondary sources, his research was pioneering in that it was the first work specifically on anarchism—highlighting a definite strand of libertarian praxis in New Zealand that has long been overlooked. Yet as Prebble notes in the introduction, "this pamphlet is not complete, much of the information is very fragmentary and a lot more work needs to be done."[7]

Apart from the relatively small number of its adherents, one of the reasons that early anarchism in New Zealand has been inadequately studied, and why further research is difficult, is due to the lack of historical records:

> a great deal of material has simply been lost due to the transitory characteristics of events. Those who were active in personal discussions and other forms of activism in their dynamic, often convulsing, and ever changing world often did not see the need or lacked the literacy to be able to document their ideas... what is left as source material are the thoughts only of those who were literate, who spoke loudly enough to be documented by others, or who wished to make themselves heard in a more durable way.[8]

Another factor that has limited some past anarchist historiography is the tendency to view its subject/s solely within national boundaries. Anarchism was a transnational movement—built upon global economic integration and both formal and informal networks crossing national lines.[9] When framed within geographical limits, anarchism in New Zealand certainly appears submerged in a sea of 'pink' socialism, even insignificant. Yet a transnational lens allows New Zealand anarchists to be viewed as part of a wider, international movement, spurred on by transoceanic migration, doctrinal diffusion, financial flows, transmission of information and symbolic practices, and acts of solidarity.[10] The role of New Zealand anarchism, both in the New Zealand labour movement and its own international movement, increases in scope when placed in such a context.

With that in mind, and by drawing on the work of Prebble and others, this contribution will explore early anarchism in New Zealand through a biography of one of its key players.[11] The transnational nature of anarchism in the period between its emergence in the workers' movement of the late 1860s and the interwar years can be seen in the migration and activity of Philip Josephs (1876–1946). His sustained activism, whether from the soapbox or through the mailbox, and his involvement in the class struggle that swept through the country, makes Josephs one of New Zealand's most important and pioneering anarchists.

As well as providing previously unpublished biographical information on Josephs, I hope to convince the reader of three main claims. Firstly, before the arrival of Josephs in New Zealand, the "broad anarchist tradition"—defined by Michael Schmidt and Lucien van der Walt as a revolutionary form of libertarian socialism against social and economic hierarchy (specifically capitalism and the state), in favour of international class struggle and revolution from below, in order to create a socialist, stateless social order—had next to no organized presence.[12] There were anarchists and various forms of anti-authoritarian ideas in New Zealand before Josephs, but it was his activity within the New Zealand Socialist Party and his formation of one of New Zealand's first anarchist collectives, the Freedom Group, that ensured a level of organized anarchism previously lacking in the wider labour movement.

The second point is one of legitimacy. Anarchism was a valid part of the New Zealand labour movement and its working-class counterculture—directly through the activity of Philip Josephs and other anarchists, or indirectly due to anarchist literature and ideas. Although often missing from the indices of New Zealand labour histories, Erik Olssen notes that anarchism was "more influential than most have realised."[13] Josephs' anarchist communism reflects the rejection of violent individualism (known as propaganda by the deed) and the move back to collective action taken by the majority of anarchists in the late 1890s. His tireless distribution of anarchist literature, numerous public speeches and his tailor-shop-cum bookshop helped to create a radical counterculture in New Zealand, while his support of syndicalist class struggle and the general strike, and his activity alongside the local branches of the Industrial Workers of the World highlights the relationship of anarchism with revolutionary syndicalism. Indeed, if one went so far as employing Schmidt and van der Walt's definition of syndicalism being a variant and strategy of the broad anarchist tradition, the era of the New Zealand Federation of Labor of 1908–1913 could be seen in a whole new light.[14]

Finally, New Zealand anarchists, and Josephs in particular, were rooted in the international anarchist movement. Josephs' birth in Latvia, his ongoing radicalisation in Glasgow, Scotland, and his almost two decades in New Zealand before he left for Australia, highlights the transient nature of labour. His distribution of international anarchist literature, and personal networking with overseas revolutionaries and groups such as Freedom Press (UK) and the Mother Earth Publishing Association (USA), illustrates the doctrinal diffusion and sharing of information so vital to informal, intercontinental anarchist networks. This sharing went both ways. Josephs' activities, the perceived bankruptcy of the Liberal Government's state-socialist legislation, and accounts of New Zealand strikes popped up on the pages of various anarchist journals abroad, lending weight to the notion that anarchism

was not a Western European doctrine that diffused outwards, perfectly formed, to a passive 'periphery.' Rather, the movement emerged simultaneously and transnationally, created by interlinked activists on many continents—a pattern of interconnection, exchange and sharing, rooted in 'informal internationalism.'[15]

Josephs played a key role in the establishment of a distinct anarchist identity and culture (in New Zealand and abroad), a culture that emerged around and enveloped the globe simultaneously. His New Zealand activity personifies the transnationalism of the day, and illustrates how interlinked (and often unrecognized) activists operating within small local scenes, but with an eye towards international developments, advanced the anarchist project worldwide. As a result, Josephs' struggle for social change linked the South Pacific nation to the global movement, and furthered anarchism in New Zealand itself—the Freedom Group of 1913 being one of the first of many anarchist collectives to play a vibrant part in the history of the New Zealand left.

CHAPTER 1

RISING EXPECTATIONS AND DASHED HOPES

The casual observer could be forgiven for reading in Philip Josephs' 1926 naturalisation papers nothing more than an Eastern European immigrant looking for the stability and closure of citizenship. Occupation: tailor; Height: 5'9"; Colour of Hair: grey; Colour of Eyes: brown; Any special Peculiarities: a bit round shoulders [sic]; Place of birth: Latvia; Children: eight. Do you swear to be faithful and bear true allegiance to His Majesty King George the Fifth and his heirs and successors, according to law? yes.[1] The reader, and the bureaucrat wielding the stamp, could never know that from the very hand that supplied these details had come powerful and unrepentant denunciations of government in all its forms, calls to go beyond man-made laws that served one class above another, and the propagation of social revolution. Indeed, the photographs of an aged Josephs that have come to light portray an avuncular, friendly demeanour—his thick, wavy, white hair framing a kind and gentle face that, according to his grandchildren, would always greet them with a smile on visits to his Sydney tailor shop. Yet as an anarchist communist and co-founder of one of New Zealand's first anarchist collectives, Josephs had forcefully agitated against all forms of authority and did not hesitate to meet ideological fire with fire. Between the lines of his naturalisation papers lies a tale of struggle for social change; a life lived through revolutionary times and bitter upheavals. Between the lines lies a biography of one of New Zealand's most consistent, pioneering, and pivotal anarchists.

Philip Josephs (Feivel Ben Yacov in his native language) was born in the Latvian port city of Liepaja (Libau) on 25 November 1876. Apart from this, there is very little information about Josephs' family, his upbringing, and what caused him to leave for Glasgow, Scotland at around twenty years of age. Some educated guesses can be employed however, for Liepaja was not free of the persecution inflicted on the wider Jewish population by the Russian government—persecution that produced violence, massive migrations, and the seeds of revolutionary thought.

Situated in southwest Latvia and straddling the Baltic Sea, the port city of Liepaja—known as 'the city where the wind is born' due to its trademark coastal breeze—was the third largest city in Latvia. Along its spacious but busy harbour were rows and rows of warehouses, bordered by unbroken white dunes and sandy shores. Unlike neighbouring ports of Riga and St. Petersburg, Liepaja remained ice-free during the winter months, making it a crucial site for the shipment of goods and capital. Its geographical importance was bolstered by the arrival of the railway in 1880, confirming the port as a significant economic centre for both Russian merchants and the Jewish community. By 1897, Liepaja had become the second largest Jewish port community in the Baltic.[2]

Life for a Jew in Liepaja was more stable and less restricted than for most in Latvia. Jewish merchants contributed to the thriving portside economy, and as a result, were allowed to reside outside the so-called Pale of Settlement—a band of territory made up of shtetls (small towns) and inner-city ghettos in which Jewish communities were normally forced to reside. In Liepaja, Jews "were free to trade and achieved a degree of cultural assimilation with their gentile neighbours that distinguished them from their Yiddish-speaking co-religionists in the Pale."[3] There were public Jewish schools for both boys and girls, a Talmud Torah (school focussing on rabbinical teachings for students of modest means), and prior to 1893, an influential Rabbinical School.[4] The cultural influence of German Jewry was present, and as well as more traditional religious bodies, institutions dedicated to the ideas of the Haskalah movement—enlightenment values, the study of secular subjects, and assimilation—could also be found in the city.[5]

Modernisation, combined with the influence of Haskalah, meant "more and more young Jews began to aspire to a secular education and a place in the general society."[6] However, the Russian government, and Alexander III's reign (1881–1894) in particular, ensured that discrimination, repression, and violence were part-and-parcel of Jewish life. Jews were restricted from certain occupations, universities, and geographical movement. The laws designed to restrict Jews to designated areas made travel especially precarious—one man, who had left his place of residence for a few days in order to get married, "was described on his return as a 'new arrival' and was consequently expelled [from the town]."[7]

These "dark clouds of reaction shrouded the [entire] country," and despite their relative freedom, the Jews of Liepaja did not completely escape the turmoils of their co-religionists.[8] As well as the denial of other rights, Jewish children, unlike their gentile playmates, were forbidden to play on the sands of Liepaja's shores. It seems they could only experience the shoreline when they were stepping off it; in 1890, the Tsarist regime enforced the Regulations on Passports, expelling large numbers of Liepaja's Jews who were not registered in the census of 13 April 1835.

Before the turn of the twentieth century, this empire of the tsars underwent "a vigorous period of challenge and upheaval" characterised by violence, a growing interest in socialism, and a fledgling labour movement, "created by the state as a by-product of its large-scale industrialisation program of the nineties."[9] It was in this atmosphere of "rising expectations and dashed hopes" that Josephs would have received some kind of education.[10] It was also this clash of modernism and repression that gave rise to Algemeyner Yidisher Arbeter Bund in Lite, Poyln un Rusland (The General Union of Jewish Workers in Lithuania, Poland, and Russia), known simply as the Bund. Officially formed in 1897, the Bund was a classical Marxist organization that sought to organize Jewish workers across the Russian empire. Its Marxist outlook meant the Bund was critical of Jewish traditionalism, especially Zionism—believing the idea of a Jewish state in Palestine was escapist and utopian. The Bund "also opposed the revival of the Hebrew language, as most Jews spoke Yiddish, and Bund members, being atheists, believed that religious books in Hebrew were not needed anyhow."[11] At one stage the membership of the Bund exceeded 30,000, but their cultural and social impact was much larger due to their populist propaganda and involvement in a number of significant strikes.

The conditions of economic stress and overt oppression also gave rise to a strong nihilist sentiment among workers, students, and peasants—a radicalism that led to the rejection of social democratic organizations (such as the Bund) in favour of more direct political action. The Bund's opposition to individual acts of violence helped to ferment "small groups of young rank-and-file Bundists [who] formed a radical 'opposition' within the movement and proclaimed a program of 'direct action' against the state and private property."[12] In the eyes of the nihilists, social democrats and their organizations were too intellectual, too reformist, and too accommodating of the state—a movement locked in a "mighty torrent of words" that lacked action and neglected anyone who was not a skilled or educated worker.[13] They increasingly "accused all the socialist groups of temporizing with the existing social system. The old order was rotten, they argued; salvation could be achieved only by destroying it root and branch. Gradualism or reformism in any shape was utterly futile."[14] Such a critique led the proponents of total revolution away from the Marxists of the Bund, and towards the ideas of Mikhail Bakunin and Pytor Kropotkin—two Russian proponents of the flowering international anarchist movement.

Although the Bund and the anarchist movement crystallized in Liepaja after Josephs' departure, the circulation of revolutionary material, radical reading and discussion circles, and the social conditions that created the Bund would have permeated his youth: "there was virtually no way a Jewish youngster could escape appreciating the civil liabilities of his Jewishness or avoid a sense of outrage."[15] Likewise, the Latvian anarchist movement, which came into existence in 1906 as a result of the abortive 1905 Russian Revolution—such as the 'Pats, Vards un Darbs!' (The Same, in Word and Deed!) Group—missed Josephs by ten years.[16] Yet his lived experience surely moulded his outlook on the nature of government and the state, creating a space that anarchism would later fill.

Indeed, around the time Josephs was coming of age, waves of mob violence directed against Jewish communities swept through the Russian empire, leading to government-sanctioned torment and terror. "While the immediate plan may have been the seizure of Jewish property," notes Kenneth Collins, "the action quickly turned to murder, rape and child mutilation."[17] As William Fishman explains, the Tsarist regime used the pogroms as an "in-built safety valve" and "turned them to their own political advantage. In a climate of growing political opposition, the pent-up hatred and frustrations of the peasantry could be diverted to a ready-made scapegoat—the Jew."[18]

Draconian laws, and a blind-eye to the pogroms, meant the Russian government succeeded in making the Jewish position in the empire altogether untenable. "Crowded into ghettos, subjected to religious persecution, largely barred from higher education and professional careers, their traditional occupations increasingly circumscribed, the Jews faced the total collapse of their economic and social structure."[19] As a result, the exodus of exploited Jews reached massive proportions, and although emigration from Russia without an exit permit was technically forbidden, "the authorities placed few obstacles in the way of would-be Jewish émigrés."[20]

For the desperate who fled the Tsarist regime and anti-Semitic violence, Liepaja was the first point of departure. Travel from Latvia was becoming more and more integrated with the wider world, and emigration from Liepaja was less arduous than from other ports. Russian gendarmes were particularly open to bribery, medical examination was less rigorous, and Western officials rarely policed access to the vessels moored in Liepaja's Winter Habour.[21] Its railway connections to wider Russia further solidified the port's role as the central departure point for emigrants making the direct journey to South Africa or America.

However, many Jews preferred the three- to five-day journey to Britain, which was cheaper than the direct route to the 'New World.' The journey may have been cheaper, but it came with a different price. Once through Russian customs (still a feat in itself) immigrants faced a sojourn riddled with sickness, overcrowding, and filthy, cattle-like conditions. On a voyage lasting from forty to sixty hours depending on the weather, passengers were herded together and made to sleep on fouled rags, dirty blankets, or in the small spaces between decks. As Rose Robins, a member of the London anarchist group Arbeter Fraynd (Workers' Friend), later recalled:

> all of us slept overcrowded in bunks, stretched side by side over the whole length of the ship. We lived in hot, stuffy, filthy conditions. We ate salt herring out of barrels distributed by ordinary seamen. My young brother, one year old, was sea sick, in agony all the time. We scratched while we slept. For the nights were a nightmare.[22]

Despite the ordeal, the desire to escape Russia and the possibilities of a new life free of discrimination meant aliens arriving in Britain from Liepaja rose from 429 in 1893 to 5,805 in 1897.[23] And Philip Josephs was one of them. Around 1897, Glasgow, the centre of Scottish radicalism, became his new home.

CHAPTER 2

GLASGOW AND THE ANARCHISTS

Although the most favoured route across Britain for those America-bound was from Hull to Liverpool, a significant number of migrants travelled across Scotland after arriving at the ports of Leith or Dundee.[1] Glasgow—the "industrial powerhouse of the Scottish economy"—became an important staging post for these travellers, and many stayed, drawn to the opportunities of a developing city and a thriving Jewish community with its own shops, synagogues, and culture.[2] Indeed, Glasgow had the third largest Jewish population in the United Kingdom, rising from 2,000 in 1891 to 6,000 a decade later.[3]

It is uncertain whether Glasgow was Josephs' intended destination, if he travelled alone, and when he arrived. The only clue to his permanency in Glasgow is permanency of another kind—on 27 November 1897, he married Sophia Hillman at the Haskalah-influenced Clyde Terrace Synagogue, in the neighbourhood of Gorbals. Sophia had also come from Latvia, born in 1876 in the south-eastern city of Daugavpils (Dzvinsk), and despite the distance between cities, it is possible she had known Josephs outside of Scotland. A rare photograph of a youthful Sophia gives the studio address as Kornstrasse, a main street in Liepaja. According to living relatives, Sophia and Philip may have arrived in Glasgow together via Germany.

One thing is certain: a mere paragraph does not do justice to Sophia's own story of struggle. Twenty-five years and a life of migration later, another photograph of Sophia with her youngest child, Edie, shows a "beautiful, elegant (did Philip make her clothing?), strong, intelligent woman, with a touch of ironic humour in her face. But an exhausted look too."[4] Two major migrations (with a third to come), a life of raising eight children, and her support of Philip and his endeavours—as well as his tribulations—are marked on Sophia's brow.

Whether Sophia and Philip romanced on a busy Latvian street or on their oceanic escape, Glasgow became their new home—Philip as a tailor and Sophia, like a number of other Jewish women, as a maker of 'top quality' cigarettes.[5] Alongside their waged work, these two new arrivals to Gorbals could soon add another task to their daily lives: parenthood. Sophia was pregnant when the couple married, and in 1898, the birth of Jeannie Josephs signalled the first of four daughters born in Glasgow before 1903.[6]

If Josephs was not already a convinced Bundist or anarchist and had left Latvia agnostic to radical politics, there were plenty of factors in Glasgow ready to convert him to the revolutionary faith of anarchism. Gorbals, south of the River Clyde and in walking distance of the city centre, was at that time, a slum. The rapid expansion of industry, coupled with its overcrowded workers' dwellings, made it one of Glasgow's grittiest neighbourhoods, littered with four-storey brick tenements shaped by the needs of the Industrial Revolution (rather than its workers). Tenants, who were unable to afford rent elsewhere, crowded into dark, unsanitary homes at a rate of more than three people to a room, resulting in regular outbreaks of smallpox and other diseases (including the bubonic plague in 1899).[7] "The common accompaniments of Gorbals life were poverty, poor housing, and ill health," confirms Collins, and although some Gorbals streets were relatively wide and prosperous, most were "repositories of filth and the breeding ground of despair and disease."[8]

Working conditions were no better. "In seeking a job," explains Fishman, "the immigrant found himself faced with a number of harsh realities. Opportunities were strictly limited. The system was periodically choked with high static and frictional unemployment. Language and cultural differences bred suspicion and hostility."[9] This, and the difficulty of adjusting to their new environment, led immigrants into a life of labour that involved unskilled and semi-skilled trades such as tailoring, "a new industry of cheap ready-made clothing to meet the demands of a 'huge and constantly increasing class who have… wide wants and narrow means.'"[10] Together with thousands of other Jewish immigrants with limited capital but plenty of labour power, Philip could soon list tailor as his occupation.

In the hope of becoming a semi-skilled machinist or even a master tailor, new immigrants in the tailoring trade (or 'greeners' as they were called) entered into a life of speedy production and tedious toil:

They started as under-pressers or plain-machinists, working for about six months for a skilled presser or machinist, doing the first preparatory work for him, till they learned the work them-selves. This lower grade of worker was employed and paid not by the master-tailor, but by the presser or machinist. Sometimes a presser or machinist employed three or four under-pressers or plain-machinists. It suited the master-tailor, because it placed the responsibility for driving the workers of the upper grade on the workers themselves... contrived [so] that each drove everybody else... it was a vicious circle, each trying to squeeze as much as possible out of those under them.[11]

Like his fellow Jewish workers in London's East End, Josephs' occupation of tailoring (by far the biggest occupation of that Jewish community) in which sweating—home workshops that exploited cheap and migrant labour—was endemic. Sweated workshops ranged from large manufacturing plants to small family businesses "working from their own usually inadequate apartments."[12] Groups of workers were huddled into often unsanitary, unventilated, and unlit rooms, and forced to perform a certain section of the production process repeatedly—effectively cutting labour costs and the need for skilled workers. Many women, desperate for work, accepted the lowest and most menial tailoring tasks without pay, hoping that at the end of their 'trial period' they would be given paid employment. But when "the so-called training time was nearly complete and perhaps work was slacker these girls would be dismissed and a new set of novices employed."[13] Likewise, the myth that by turning one's living room into a workshop and with the help of family, the Jewish tailor could 'become master' was mostly that: a myth. "Only a ruthless minority made it... the majority who tried, suffered their dubious hour of glory as master, then sank back into poverty and debt."[14]

Organizations were created to fight such conditions. In the aftermath of an explosive wildcat strike against sweating by 10,000 tailors in the East End, a Jewish Tailors Union was formed in Glasgow, which soon joined the Trades Council in 1890 as the Amalgamated Jewish Tailors, Machinists and Pressers Union.[15] Friendly societies that catered to workers were also active in the Jewish community, such as the Poalei Tsedek (Workingmen's Synagogue), the Jewish Working Men's Club, and the Jewish Workers' Co-operative Society—made possible due to a weakening of religious traditionalism.[16] Many Eastern European Jews brought the influence of the Bund with them, while evening English classes, a Literary Society, and public lectures all contributed to an embracing of "mainstream Scottish working-class values and culture" open to addressing the questions of the day.[17]

Those who confronted sweating and the inequalities of late-nineteenth-century society more vigorously than others, were anarchists. For adherents such as Bakunin and Kropotkin, these inequalities were the result of exploitative social relationships; sweating, alienation, wage-slavery, and the unequal distribution of wealth in society was the natural result of capitalism and its relations of production. In this regard, anarchists were little different than other socialists. What differentiated figures like Bakunin and Kropotkin from their comrades in the wider socialist movement was their understanding of hierarchy: power relations of authority that allowed an individual to be controlled by another. This violence of coercive authority and domination in all aspects of life—such as personal relations between men and women, between races, in education and the family, and in collective organizations such as unions—was denounced by anarchists as unjust, unnecessary, and harmful.

The epitome of hierarchy and coercive authority, and the focal point of much anarchist agitation, was the state: a power structure (whether liberal, socialist, or Marxist) they believed not only served as capital's lackey, but also hindered individual freedom and the development of real social wealth. Instead, anarchists sought to replace capitalism and the state with a social order based on co-operation, the voluntary co-ordination of common interests, and non-hierarchical relations. Far from advocating chaos, Emma Goldman—a staunch feminist and tireless campaigner for social justice—argued that such a social order would guarantee "every human being free access to the earth and full enjoyment of the necessities of life," a life free of domination, class division, and exploitation.[18]

How that society would actually function, and what tactics would be used to get there, usually depended on the individual's personal position and the particular developmental stage of anarchism. The various branches of the anarchist family tree were generally summarised as individualist, collectivist, or communist, and each gave rise to their own thinkers and tactics (although such positions were far from homogenous). However, the most predominant form of anarchism (what Schmidt and van der Walt term 'the broad anarchist tradition') had a mass social base, one that "emphasized positive, constructive activism—organizing clubs, neighbourhoods, workers' cooperatives, experimental schools, collective farms, mutual-aid societies, and anarcho-syndicalist labour unions."[19] Far from being allergic to organization, mass anarchists advocated a kind of organization from below, and threw themselves headfirst into the debates of the International Workingmen's Association (IWA, or the First International). As a result, the broad anarchist tradition—which included the anarchist communism of Josephs—was firmly rooted in the workers' movement of the 1860s. From then on, anarchism as a working class ideology became a thorn in the side of capital and the state across the globe, whether in Switzerland or Spain, Korea or Argentina—or in this case, Scotland and New Zealand.

Glasgow and its outer limits (such as Paisley) had active anarchist groups and militants whose own development had roots in the increasingly anti-parliamentary Socialist League. Spurred on by Kropotkin's 1886 visit and the powerful words of American anarchist Lucy Parsons (1888), the local branch of the Socialist League progressively turned "in the Anarchist direction," which—according to one of the League's prominent figures, William Morris—gave them "an agreeable air of toleration."[20] A parting with the League took place in late 1892 or early 1893, with the anarchists finally coalescing into the Glasgow Anarchist Group in October 1893. By March 1894, a member stated that they had "five times the members we started with," and were propagating the principles of anarchy at such a rate that anarchists were barred from speaking at Labour Party discussions.[21] The Group held numerous outdoor meetings against the Boer War (1899–1902), distributed literature, and co-operated with the Paisley Group to publish the syndicalist-inspired newspaper *Voice of Labour* in January 1904.[22]

During this time Glasgow continued to be frequented by international anarchists thanks to the connections of two of the Group's members, William and Maggie Duff. It was the Duffs who played host to another American anarchist, Voltairine de Cleyre, during her tours of Scotland in September 1897 and August/September 1903; could count anarchists such as the geographer Élisée Reclus, Goldman, and Kropotkin as friends; and penned articles in international journals such as San Francisco's anarchist communist newspaper, *Free Society*.[23] An anarchist bookstore in the centre of the city also helped contribute to the spread of anarchism in Glasgow, and London—a mecca of European anarchism—was a mere train ride away. London-based anarchists such as Rudolf Rocker often gave lectures in Glasgow, packing halls with discussions on the Russian pogroms and sweating in the East End.

Rocker's connection to the Jewish anarchists of London was particularly fruitful. After moving to the city from Paris, the popular figure and captivating orator joined the Arbeter Fraynd group, a Jewish anarchist collective based in the East End that also produced a newspaper of the same name. Mainly edited by Rocker and written entirely in Yiddish, the Arbeter Fraynd covered local and international labour news, tirelessly called for unity between Jewish and English workers, and put forward the ideas and tactics of anarchism—all designed to use the immigrant worker's Jewish identity as a springboard for solidarity and class struggle. The paper also concerned itself with combating Marxism in the Jewish labour movement, publishing twenty-five essays by Rocker alone on the subject. As a result, Rocker and the Arbeter Fraynd contained some of the earliest critiques of Marxism and historical materialism in Yiddish (a theme that would later be explored by Josephs and his Freedom Group comrades).[24]

As well as their newspaper, the Arbeter Fraynd collective also helped to translate anarchist books and pamphlets into the language of the Jewish immigrant. One such pamphlet was a comprehensive, twenty-two page exposition of anarchist communism in Yiddish that was later translated into German, French, and Dutch.[25]

Alongside the spreading of anarchist literature, the Jewish anarchists had their own hall, complete with a library, meeting spaces, and a bar. Events such as anarchist Yom Kippur balls—"featuring dancing, merry-making, and atheistic harangues"—would be organized to clash with traditional Jewish festivities, attracting the attention of non-religious Jews and the scorn of the faithful.[26] As Rocker put it, "the place for believers was the house of worship, and the place for non-believers was the radical meeting."[27]

For many Jewish radicals, anarchism meant a complete rejection of religion. "Just as every state, they argued, was an instrument by which a privileged few wielded power over the immense majority, so every church was an ally of the state in the subjugation of humanity."[28] Yet for some, the boundaries of anarchism and Judaism were blurred. "Anarchism, for all its international pretensions... has always been divided into national and ethnic groups," argues Paul Avrich. This sense of ethnicity was possible because "anarchists, cherishing diversity against standardization and uniformity, have always prized the differences among peoples—cultural, linguistic, historical—quite as much as their common bonds."[29] Many Jewish anarchists embraced an atheism that retained a sense of their Jewish cultural diversity—without observing its orthodox traditionalism. For others, anarchism was the natural extension of a radical Judaism "deeply motivated by ethical questions, incensed by injustices. They carried a very Jewish sense of righteousness."[30] The "new rabbis of liberty" strove to show that, in practice, Jewish anarchism was not a contradiction in terms.[31]

Atheism aside, cultural and material commonalities were an important link for Jewish anarchists and their fellow workers. As well as encouraging them to question the fetters of traditionalism and to join the anarchist counter-culture, orators such as Rocker went to the workers themselves—endlessly organizing Jewish labourers knee deep in sweated shirts. A demonstration of 25,000 against the pogroms in Russia, and a nationwide conference of Jewish anarchists in December 1902, confirmed the fruits of their labour. Alongside Jewish anarchist movements in the US and elsewhere, Rocker and the Arbeter Fraynd collective had fostered the growth of a unique, widely embraced, and long-lasting Jewish anarchist identity. In the British Isles, such an identity was not restricted to London's East End. According to Collins there were also Jewish anarchists in Glasgow itself, and as Rocker notes in *The London Years*, "our best centre after Leeds, was Glasgow."[32]

Although Josephs does not appear in the few surviving records of the Jewish Unions and anarchist groups of the day, the prevalence of anarchism in Glasgow and the work of Rocker and the Jewish anarchists in London surely confirmed Josephs' political outlook. The Duffs lived within walking distance of the Josephs household, and Glasgow Green, a popular open-air auditorium for socialists and anarchists of all shades, was a mere two blocks away. Yet even closer to home was Sophia's brother, Arthur Hillman. A founding member, with Rocker, of the Workers' Circle Friendly Society (a socialist mutual aid society designed to protect its members through times of sickness or need), a member of the Bund, and self-proclaimed anarchist, Josephs' brother-in-law preached from a pulpit radically different than family tradition (the Hillmans having produced a long line of prominent rabbanim).[33] Instead, Arthur struggled financially due to his anarchist convictions. In order to make ends meet he had a business selling 'antique rugs'—new rugs that he would beat with dirt in order to grant them antique status![34]

Another radical Bundist in the family was the cousin of Arthur and Sophia, Sidney Hillman. After being radicalised in one of the many illegal Russian study circles of the day, in 1904 Sidney led the first ever May Day march in the Lithuanian city of Kovno. For his efforts he suffered the fate of many of his comrades—imprisonment. After escaping Russia, he eventually went on to become a prominent labour leader in the New Deal era, devising America's first system of welfare as Secretary of Labor to President Franklin Roosevelt, and a key member of the Congress of Industrial Organizations.

Who radicalised whom? Was Josephs the 'bad apple' that brought anarchism into the Hillman household, influenced by the steady stream of anarchist agitation in Glasgow? Or was his anarchism the result of personal interaction with Arthur, Sidney, and Sophia? Maybe a shared adherence to anarchism was what brought Philip and Sophia together? Either way, when Philip, Sophia, and their four girls embarked for Wellington, New Zealand aboard the Prinz Regent-Luitpold late in 1903, Josephs was a convinced revolutionary—armed with mental dynamite and transnational connections.

CHAPTER 3

A WORKINGMAN'S PARADISE?

The influence Josephs had on the development of anarchism in New Zealand can be seen when his activities are placed in context. Before his arrival, there was simply no organized anarchist movement in New Zealand, and unlike its nearest neighbour Australia (which had anarchist groups as early as 1886), self-proclaimed anarchists were few and far between. As a result, the traces of anarchism in New Zealand before his arrival in 1904 come from an often-hostile press, concerned police, or in the form of a few eclectic individuals such as Arthur Desmond and Alexander Bickerton (of whom more later). And although workers' self-activity and anti-authoritarian voices are audible throughout the development of New Zealand society, I do not want to confuse "the history of the revolutionary anarchist movement with the universal history of anti-authoritarian thought"—even if such a history would be both fascinating and fruitful.[1] The pages herein deal primarily with those who, as Barry Pateman puts it, have crossed the river of fire, and identify as such.

Despite an upsurge of new unionism where workers "began to see themselves as representatives of a class rather than a craft or trade" (culminating in the national Maritime Strike of 1890), New Zealand at the turn of the twentieth century has predominately been viewed as a 'Workingman's Paradise.'[2] The arcadian imagery of New Zealand that was sold to its early immigrants—a 'land of milk and honey' where natural abundance and the innate moderation of its inhabitants would abolish the necessity for social organization and its by-products of wealth, power, and status—has lingered on, partly because the workers who packed up and left the Old World did not want to admit that their sacrifices had been in vain, and also because "powerful mechanisms prevented the formation of alternative and contrasting visualisations."[3]

Historical narratives are one such mechanism. In Miles Fairburn's *The Ideal Society and its Enemies*, casualized labour relationships and mobility between employment; the prevalence of the individualist, nomadic, and transient single male; and a minimal development of working class communities (or cohesive social organization in general), are upheld to illustrate that New Zealand society, at least before 1890, was relatively free of hierarchy and class divisions.[4] One historian even goes so far as to ask whether New Zealanders "have or have had a bourgeoisie and a proletariat, and a struggle between the two."[5] Relatively progressive laws, coupled with perceived egalitarian attitudes of the population, led historians and contemporaries alike to promote the country as an equal society: a land without strikes.[6] From 1894, when legislation was introduced that outlawed strike action and forced unions and employers into negotiated industrial awards governed by the Arbitration Court (known as the Industrial Conciliation and Arbitration Act, or ICA), until a strike by Auckland tramway workers in 1906, there were no recorded strikes in New Zealand.

Yet such a view conveniently precludes the existence of class struggle outside of strike action, and essentially dismisses the possibility of an anarchist movement in New Zealand. The notion that the colony was free of class and hierarchy also neglects the fact that New Zealand's western culture was founded on the destruction, exploitation, and colonization of the local indigenous population and their resources. And while it is true that before 1904 explicitly anarchist activity is minimal, it hides the fact that from the arrival of its very first settlers in the early-nineteenth century, New Zealand has been a capitalist society—divided by class and informed by social relations of production and accumulation in both urban and rural New Zealand. Hierarchy, gender division, the subordination of all aspects of life to work, and the constant reproduction of capital is intertwined with such relations, and whether those relationships were casualized, sporadic, or isolated does not negate their existence. Even if workers had managed to avoid the wage relation for a short time (and worked for themselves), wage relations dominated the wider society in which that labour was per-formed. "Capitalism is not just a social system that exploits people through work," but does so through its ability "to turn all of life into work for its own reproduction."[7] In other words, individuals—directly or indirectly—were always dominated by capitalist relations. As one of the world's youngest colonies, New Zealand was no exception.

It is clear that the global reproduction of capital was a driving factor in the colonization of New Zealand. Capitalist relations were "trans-planted quite deliberately by the sponsors of the New Zealand Company," an organization that competed with the British government in the quest to monopolize New Zealand pastures. In response to the American and Australian example, and in order to give capital the opportunity to accumulate in New Zealand, the director of the company, Edward Gibbon Wakefield, repeatedly argued that:

> the ruling authority should put a high price on virgin land so that the labourer would have to work a considerable time before he could save enough to become a landowner... before he withdrew[from the labour market] he would have to work long enough to provide capital accumulation for the original landowning employers and to save a sum to provide a fund to bring out other wage workers to take his place.[8]

Accordingly, land prices were kept high to ensure a class of labourers, agricultural mechanics, and domestic servants would be available for exploitation by landowners who remained home in England, helping to cement "not a subsistence but a capitalist economy."[9] This economy, geared to provide British capital with fruits from New Zealand's "quarry of stored-up natural resources," relied on the suppression of Maori and the labour power of the working class.[10] As a result, New Zealand soon featured the evils many immigrants thought they had left at the docks: wage labour, want in a land of plenty, strikes, and unemployment. The withdrawal of labour as acts of protest broke out in 1821, 1840, and again in 1841, and as early as 1877, large meetings of the unemployed could be found on the street corners of the colony.[11]

If class was solely based on income (which it is not), one could also point out that between 1903 and 1904, 0.5 percent of the New Zealand population owned 33 percent of its wealth.[12] Stevan Eldred-Grigg in *New Zealand Working People* notes that many landowners earned £20,000 to £30,000 a year, often tax free, while the wages of a farm labourer were £41 per year. Female nursemaids working the same estate house sometimes earned as little as £13 annually. While an idle few pocketed huge fortunes, such as Sir George Clifford and his £512,000 worth of assets (over 30,000 times the average working wage), the majority worked, and worked hard—a simple commodity in the eyes of some employers. "I just look on them as I do on a bag of potatoes," claimed one factory owner.[13] Again, it was worse if you were female. When the Wellington Domestic Workers' Union asked the Arbitration Court for the hours worked by maids to be reduced to sixty-eight a week, they were turned away.

There is no doubting the fact that early colonial New Zealand was a considerable improvement on the Old World, that individualism was the prevalent ideology, and that some immigrants did find relative freedom when compared with their past lives. "It is clear that there was a high degree of transience and that the working class was fragmented in New Zealand," writes Melanie Nolan, "fragmented by sex and race into pockets, and by the smallest of workplaces and communities."[14] But this does not equal a society without class. Likewise, the colony may have been free of recorded strikes for a short period, but it was never without capitalist relations—locally or globally. No amount of state liberalism in the form of women's suffrage, pensions, or law-locked unions could ever abolish hierarchy, class, and gender divisions. In reality, these reforms were the direct response of capital to the resistance of New Zealand workers in the late 1880s, and while they certainly improved some aspects of working life, they simply helped file down the rough edges of capitalism's chains. As Edward Tregear, ex-Secretary of the Labour Department, wrote: "there had been a feeling (perhaps unconscious) that they [the Government] had to settle every [Parliamentary] Session with how few bones could be thrown to the growling Labour Dog to keep him from actually biting."[15]

Alongside class divisions and an overarching state, Victorian ideology, religion, and the interests of the press heavily influenced the 'Britain of the South.' Although its power was watered down due to the lack of any official church, and despite some clergymen supporting liberal causes, religion—in a range of denominations—played a strong role in maintaining certain standards of behaviour in the colony. Churches were often a voice for moral controls over the wider population, and helped to push through parliament "some of the empire's strictest Sabbatarian laws."[16] Likewise, for a population that depended on newspapers for much of its information, the press tended towards the prevailing views of the status quo and were often open to expressing the views of the mainstream Protestant churches—churches that were generally suspicious of socialism. In the eyes of most clergy, anarchism was seen as "a dangerous atheistic creed."[17]

Yet despite such factors (or because of them), there existed an anti-authoritarian instinct that Eldred-Grigg insists came close to the spirit of anarchism:

> Anarchism was deeply rooted in the instincts of working people. Bureaucracy, the state, the whole business of government, seemed alien and inimical. Dislike of government was linked with a strong preference for a world of ease, a world where people chin-wagged rather than hectored, where spaces were small and relationships close. Working people frequently felt contempt for what a union leader described as 'that political box of tricks called Parliament'… anarchism was not so much a political movement as a feeling that the state and big business represented the world of 'them' not 'us'.[18]

Pierre-Joseph Proudhon's slogan 'Property is Theft' was so popular in 1890, writes Eldred-Grigg, "that one wealthy landowner took pains to repudiate it as 'cant' [mere jargon]."[19] Whether it was used in full sincerity is open to debate, but at the very least, the men and women whose lives revolved around labour, or who did not own property, knew that New Zealand was far from a workingman's (or woman's) paradise.

Those who owned the country's newspapers certainly strove to portray the harmony of capitalist social relations in the colony, and despite a few exceptions, anarchist thought was either reported negatively or overwhelmingly denounced. As early as 1840, the seemingly delayed colonization of New Zealand was said to be promoting 'anarchy' by some commentators: "unless immediate steps be taken to establish the complete administration of British law in New Zealand, it is greatly to be feared that the large and respectable body of Her Majesty's subjects who have lately proceeded thither will be placed in a state of anarchy, and subjected to great evils accordingly."[20] Reports of the 1848 French Revolution carried the exploits of 'anarchist leaders', and as well as tirades on the Paris Commune, the year 1871 featured a local letter in the *Evening Post* titled "Revolutionary Anarchism" that confusedly advocated the ideas of Italian Republican Giuseppe Mazzini.[21] Sensationalist articles in the early 1880s, such as "Anarchism, Socialism, and Nihilism," "Nihilism: What is It?," and "Socialists in London," painted the ideas of Bakunin, Johann Most, and other "extreme anarchists" in a negative light, warning the good citizens of New Zealand that "the quarrel of the Anarchist is with human society itself, and that is a quarrel that may be prosecuted as fitly in New Zealand as in Paris or Chicago."[22]

Anarchism as a scourge against society was a reoccurring theme. In 1894, Wellington audiences enjoyed a public lecture on "Anarchism: Its Origin and Aim" by Liberal politician and lawyer, Sir John George Findlay. Although he shared Proudhon quotes with his listeners and mentioned anarchist "writers of such ability in literature and science as Kropotkin and Reclus," Findlay peppered his presentation with rhetoric designed to darken the imagination. Anarchists were part of "the horde of idle loafers who form the dregs of every State... whose degradation and poverty are but the wages of their own intemperance and idleness"; while anarchism itself "aims at annihilation of all external authority and is avowedly a declaration of war against every social institution... to destroy by every possible means this cursed growth we call society." "The blind enthusiasts," concluded Findlay, "would hasten on the wheels of human progress by the bomb, the pistol, and the dagger." In their growth, "the death of society" drew near.[23]

Richard Hill shows that the New Zealand police shared the same perception of anarchists as the mainstream media—violent, extremist, and in need of surveillance. In 1895, "quiet enquiries were being made about a reported anarchist headquarters 'somewhere down South'. In response, Dunedin detectives reported that some radical members of the Knights of Labour [an international fraternal society that promoted the ideas of new unionism and whose membership in New Zealand reached about 5,000] had broken away to form a more 'extreme' group, but they would not 'go to the length of Anarchists.'" Police believed that "any anarchists in the colony would be in Auckland because of its hosting of 'French escapees' from New Caledonia," which seems to be confirmed by the Northern District Commander, who knew "many French and Germans with Anarchical opinions." In 1900, "an Austrian boarding house where the 'rules of Anarchists' were allegedly being studied" was under watch, and when the Duke and Duchess of Cornwall and York toured New Zealand in 1901, "all passenger vessels arriving in the colony were boarded by detectives in search of 'suspicious' persons—including those 'who may possibly be members of foreign Anarchist Societies.'"[24] When stowaways were actually found on board the *Sonoma* (a mail steamer from San Francisco), the customs report noted that they "may be anarchists."[25]

Such a response was in line with the worldwide reaction to anarchism's foray into propaganda by the deed—a complex period of activity that placed those in positions of authority on tenterhooks. Many anarchists felt "the time had come when verbal propaganda was no use any more," writes Hermia Oliver, that "it was absolutely necessary to propagate the revolutionary idea by deeds, and to arouse the spirit of revolt in sections of the masses who still had illusions about the effectiveness of legal methods."[26] From the 1870s to the turn of the century, dynamite was seen as the tool with which to corrode the chains of domination. Volleys of violence against monarchs, state officials, or employers were to "rouse the masses from their slumber," and act as retaliation for what was believed to be a wider, more degrading violence inflicted daily on workers by the capitalist class. These insurrections were "based on the belief that the revolution was near; that it would erupt spontaneously, provoked by the violent action of individuals or small groups."[27] Yet for others, propaganda of the deed was a cry of despair, having lost faith in revolution and the ability of the working class to rebel.[28]

Dynamite and anarchism soon became synonymous in the minds of the public, thanks to a sensationalist press eager to forward their accounts at the expense of analysis. For example, the assassination of US President William McKinley by Leon Czolgosz in 1901 gained considerable attention in New Zealand, prompting a discussion on anarchism in the *NZ Times*. An editorial footnote to one reader's letter ended with a provocation:

> We do not believe that there are any anarchists in New Zealand. If however, they do exist, and this should meet the eye of one or more of them, we cordially invite them to state their doctrines and designs. A bona fide anarchist, or anyone who can explain the ideas that dominate these enemies of organized society, is welcome to a column of our space to state the case for anarchism.[29]

As well as letters denouncing anarchists as 'wretched slayers' and 'murderers by nature,' a number of individuals—including future Federation of Labor (FOL) lawyer Patrick O'Regan—took up the offer and tried to differentiate the insurrectionist anarchists from those who, realizing the negative impact of such deeds, had changed tack in the late 1890s.[30] Kropotkin, Leo Tolstoy, and Herbert Spencer are mentioned as those who upheld more 'respectable' anarchist views, although in reply, S.W. Fitzherbert argued that Spencer had nothing to do with "Philosophical Anarchists" such as Proudhon, Max Stirner, Bakunin, Kropotkin, Reclus, Benjamin Tucker, and Jean Grave.[31]

This roll-call of international anarchists illustrates that early socialists in New Zealand seem to have been aware of the more faithful representations of anarchism, if only in the basic form of key individuals, or the "vaguely anarchist Socialist League."[32] As Kerry Taylor points out, theories of socialism and communism had been discussed quite early in the European history of New Zealand, and began in earnest in the 1890s.[33] Anarchism would have crossed the paths of inquisitive socialists, even if few decided to walk its thorny trails.

One defender of anarchism in the *NZ Times* was Alexander Bickerton, a professor of chemistry at Canterbury College, Christchurch. Although a self-described state socialist, on trips back to England Bickerton had met Kropotkin, the Italian anarchist Errico Malatesta, and French anarchist educationalist Paul Robin. According to Frank Prebble, Bickerton "became convinced that genuine communism would be easier to obtain than any steps taken towards it." To that end, in 1896 he established the Wainoni Federative Home in Christchurch—an experiment in communal living that lasted till around 1903 (when it became a theme park, with a zoo, cinema, and aquariums).[34] Interestingly, Robin made a brief visit to New Zealand in 1898, possibly with the view to forming an anarchist colony. However, it appears he left a few months later.[35]

Bickerton's letter in the *NZ Times* notes that he "had a good many talks with Prince Kropotkine [sic]," and quotes at length two *Freedom* pamphlets by Kropotkin and Malatesta—including a thirty-line definition of anarchist communism and a passage that both counters the 'enemy of society' stereotype and illustrates the collective nature of the broad anarchist tradition:

"No man," says Michael Bakounine [sic], "can recognize his own human worth, nor in consequence realise his full development, if he does not recognize the worth of his fellow-men, and in co-operation with them, realise his own development through them. No man can emancipate himself unless he emancipates those around him. My freedom is the freedom for all, for I am not really free—free not only in thought, but in deed—if my freedom and my right do not find their confirmation and...sanction in the liberty and right of all men and equals."[36]

Despite such lofty prose, Bickerton faced an uphill battle. One reader of the *NZ Times*, after seeing that a college professor such as Bickerton was "a confessed apostle of anarchism," exclaimed in dismay: "There are parents of students whom the unexpected statement has considerably disturbed; and what of the feelings of the other professors who have no want of social disorder?"[37]

Another figure sympathetic to the revolutionary ideas of anarchism was Arthur Desmond, a "red-bearded poet, novelist, songwriter and agitator" that, although not a self-described anarchist, deserves a mention.[38] Desmond's flamboyant and somewhat mysterious life started in Hawke's Bay, New Zealand around 1859. Before leaving the country for Australia in 1892, he had run for Parliament twice (publicly denouncing bank directors as "scoundrels," estate owners as "bloodsucking leeches," and the local press as "hirelings of monopoly"), caused a stir by supporting Maori leader and ex-guerrilla Te Kooti Arikirangi Te Turuki, and published the radical labour paper *Tribune* from a squatted office belonging to the Auckland Employers Association.[39] He helped organize Northland workers into the Gum Diggers Union, and during the 1890 Maritime Strike, was a prominent strike leader in Auckland. Later, in Australia, he was a member of the Active Service Brigade (a militant organization of the unemployed whose immediate objective was the decent accommodation of Sydney's workless until the overthrow of capitalism and the attainment of socialism) and for the remainder of his much-speculated-about life, continued to associate with revolutionaries of all shades.[40]

Despite their proximity to the country, the Active Service Brigade, the Melbourne Anarchist Club, and other Australian anarchist groups or individuals seem to have had limited interaction with New Zealand at that time. According to Australian historian Bob James, *Liberator*, the newsletter of the Australian Secular Association (whose membership included many anarchists), listed distribution agents throughout New Zealand, and Australian anarchists may have moved on from organizing in Australia to the shores of their southern neighbour.[41] But apart from Desmond's transnationalism, and without conducting extensive research in Australia, trans-Tasman anarchist links are next-to-none.

Despite the existence of capitalist relations and its by-products of class division, exploitation, and hierarchy; and despite an instinctual anti-authoritarianism, numerous press articles, and the radicalism of Bickerton and Desmond, evidence of 'bona fide' anarchists is scarce in New Zealand before 1904—not because of a supposedly arcadian society, but because individuals either did not identify as such (or they did but failed to coalesce), or due to the lack of historical records. New Zealand capitalism was still relatively young, and as an organized force, the worldwide anarchist movement was even younger. The media stereotype of the anarchist-cum-bomber that continued well into the 1920s also made it problematic for people to identify as such. Nonetheless, after the turn of the century, a rise in labour militancy and the arrival of Philip Josephs meant the anarchist communism of the latter would receive a much more balanced hearing in New Zealand.

CHAPTER 4

WELLINGTON'S WORKING-CLASS COUNTER-CULTURE

Wellington, a bustling port city of narrow streets, windy weather, and high-density housing, welcomed Philip and the family on 7 March 1904, after a brief stopover in Sydney, Australia. "Upon landing," noted the 1898 *Cyclopedia of New Zealand*, "a stranger discovered there was no very commendable foresight in the laying out of the town. The streets were too narrow, objectionably so."[1] Indeed, New Zealand's capital was squeezed between the shoreline and a looming green belt. The central city of plaster-ornamented, two- to three-storey commercial buildings surrounded by "a mosaic of one- and two-storey workers' homes, small factories [and] cottage industries," had to somehow accommodate a population that, by 1900, had doubled in size.[2] While vacant land lay idle due to a large number of absentee landowners, workers and their families were crammed into what little space was left. Narrow sections of single-storeyed, one-room-wide dwellings made of rickety timber and with rusting iron roofs sprang up between industry and its directors (who resided in the more well-to-do suburbs of Kelburn and Karori). Although not slums on the scale of Gorbals or the East End, areas such as Te Aro and Aro Valley were described as such—they often flooded with filthy waters due to inadequate drainage systems, and heavy rains spelled an increase in sewage and disease. Even in the early 1900s there were still difficulties in disposing of the city's refuse.

What prompted Philip and Sophia to take their children from Glasgow to New Zealand? And why settle in Wellington? Once again, Philip's naturalisation papers point to a possibility. When he was naturalized as a New Zealander in 1921, a woman named Betty Gordon, acting as

Josephs' referee, stated: "I have known him since he was a child. Mr. Josephs and myself were born in the same town... and I have known Mr. Josephs from the time of his arrival in New Zealand to the present date."[3] Betty was the wife of Solomon Gordon, a Russian picture framer, co-founder of the New Zealand Labour Party, and another Wellington Jew. The Gordons had also lived in Scotland—Solomon was secretary of the Independent Labour Party's Inverness Branch (and a friend of its leader James Keir Hardie) before moving to Wellington around 1901. That Josephs was from the same city as Betty, and shared a socialist connection with Solomon in Scotland, surely meant they were family friends. It is likely that the Gordons, having moved to Wellington, wrote back to Philip and Sophia in Glasgow and suggested they follow suit. For when the Gordon family packed up and shipped out to Sydney in 1921, the Josephs family went too.

In the meantime, still fresh off the boat from Glasgow, the Josephs settled down to their new environs. Their home at 43 Aro Street bordered the dwellings of Te Aro but placed them in Aro Valley—a working class suburb with an abundance of closely built houses and a reputation for political radicalism. Rather fittingly, the family arrived into their new location with a bang. A week after landing in the city, New Zealand readers received a taste of Philip's radicalism thanks to a newspaper interview he gave during his stopover in Australia. "Will the Japanese Be Beaten" in the *Wanganui Chronicle* described his opinion of Russia's war with Japan and the situation they had left behind:

> Everybody [in Russia], except the rich people, want to have things changed. The poor man is robbed, and badly treated by the police, the governors, and the rich. The students are also unjustly treated... there will soon be a change. The people will rise up and will get freedom... The Nihilists and students will not help the Government. They will not fight for them, but will soon fight for themselves. The people do not want to go to war—only the rich people.[4]

The article goes on to state that "Mr. Josephs, who is a Russian Jew... is possessed of a bitter hatred of the Russian officials and soldiers... [He said] they rob and murder women and children, and no Jews are safe. The officials encourage the soldiers in their excesses, and will not punish them."[5] It was safer for him and his family to leave.

As well as establishing a small tailor shop at 64 Taranaki Street, Josephs quickly bolstered the ranks of the city's radicals, involving himself in solidarity demonstrations against the injustices suffered by his fellow Russian workers during the 1905 Revolution. At the same time as Parisian and London workers gathered in their hundreds to hear Russian anarchists like Kropotkin speak on the massacre of Bloody Sunday and the situation in Russia, Josephs was bringing the horrors of his home-land to the workers of Wellington. On numerous occasions, Josephs publicly voiced his disgust at the oppressive nature of the Russian government—describing from the platform at one mass meeting the "wretched conditions of the Working Class in Russia."[6] "Doloi S Russki Samoderszavie!" (Down With Russian Tyranny!) also featured Josephs as a main speaker, where he "spoke with force and earnestness on the evening's theme... explaining something of the revolutionary propaganda, and describing some of the scenes of horror that incited the revolters to count no odds in their struggle for freedom."[7]

Like the early stages of the British anarchist movement, the lack of any local anarchist organization placed Josephs' activity directly in his immediate socialist milieu.[8] Luckily for Josephs, Wellington was blossoming into a centre of working-class counter-culture—a conscious community that emphasized a shared working-class identity ('we') in conflict with the imposed values and ideology of the employing class ('them'). "By emphasizing class conflict in daily life," writes Fran Shor, working class radicals developed what has been called 'counter-publics'—the building of a "proletarian public sphere where working class solidarity and emancipation were enacted in competition with bourgeois and respectable norms."[9] This complex and often contradictory sphere was based upon alternative ideas on the nature of social relationships, informal patterns of association, and the shared experience of working life. Open-air meetings such as the mass protests witnessed in Wellington were particularly important in fermenting a proletarian public sphere, as was the creation of specific institutions, rituals, and symbols.

Active in the demonstrations of Russian solidarity was one such institution, the Wellington branch of the New Zealand Socialist Party (NZSP)—a broad group of revolutionary socialists, which Josephs soon joined. Formed in July 1901 after a group of British socialists (known as the Clarion Settlers, after the British newspaper that inspired them to emigrate) failed to establish a socialist colony in New Zealand, the NZSP was a national organization that, in its early stages, encompassed a range of revolutionary positions. Its uncompromising revolutionary socialist stance, the rejection of parliamentary politics, and its sympathy to syndicalism allowed anarchists such as Josephs to share in its socialist agitation.[10]

Like Josephs, the originators of the NZSP also managed to arrive in New Zealand with accompanying headlines. According to reports, in November 1900, a 'gang' of thirty Clarion Settlers caused discord aboard the *SS Tokomaru* after clashing with some of its more patriotic passengers, including several soldiers returning from South Africa. "Persons describing themselves as Socialists and Anarchists" had insulted "British subjects and men wearing the uniform of their Queen" by raising three cheers to the Social Revolution after an onboard concert, and singing the French revolutionary anthem, the "Marsellaise." A meeting was called to protest the "wholesale importation of Anarchists, Revolutionists, and other bandits into the peace-loving and law-abiding colony of New Zealand;" to "consider what punishment was to be meted out to the Anarchists;" and to elect "five gentlemen to wait on the Premier when the boat arrived in New Zealand [explaining] to him the class of people coming out as emigrants."[11]

Yet conflicting accounts paint less acrimonious scenes. According to other passengers, the group were "the most intelligent and most behaved passengers on board," who simply spent their time debating the merits of various socialist thinkers. Instead, a personal feud between a Clarionette and another passenger had led the latter to circulate rumours "that the debaters were a band of Anarchists, holding revolutionary meetings." In response, the singing of the "Marsellaise" was meant to be a joke: "the fun was fast and furious, and greatly enjoyed by a big crowd of spectators. Eventually nearly everybody got to know and understand each other." Once ashore, Clarion emigrants jokingly explained they had been dubbed anarchists, and that "the statements made to the papers... caused both amusement and indignation to those acquainted with the actual facts."[12] While actual facts are hard to come by, it is clear that the anarchist label was already a negative one for the majority of New Zealand's citizens—readily roped around any kind of socialist rhetoric, anarchist or otherwise.

Although the Clarion Settlers' socialist colony never materialized, the presence of socialism in the country had greatly increased thanks to their arrival. By October 1901, the Wellington branch of the NZSP could claim nearly 100 members, reaching 3,000 members nationally in 1908.

The NZSP also had a significant hand in creating and fostering Wellington's working-class counter-culture. Political and cultural events, their own newspaper, the *Commonweal*, and a Socialist Hall gave the socialists a presence in the city well beyond their membership—a presence in which Josephs and his anarchism played a major part. The party's popular weekly economic classes, which included "members of Trades Unions, Single Taxers, and other sympathisers and searchers after truth" were not only initiated by Josephs, but run by him.[13] Josephs was certainly in the thick of things, for when the NZSP put out a statement in June 1905 warning fellow workers of a fraudster masquerading as a socialist organizer (who was taking subscriptions for classes and a newspaper that did not exist), Josephs was a co-signatory.[14] He also had a hand in revealing a fake doctor named 'Dr. Boranoff' who, according to Josephs' letter on the front page of the *Maoriland Worker* (the influential weekly paper of the Federation of Labor [FOL]) was actually Dr. Caplan—a petty criminal from England with shady credentials and past convictions, who had also "claimed to have been connected with the revolutionary movement in Russia." "He has not only misrepresented the Russian revolutionary movement, but grossly insulted it," exclaimed Josephs, and "all those who are interested in the welfare of the labour movement in New Zealand are warned against [him]."[15] Josephs' knowledge of socialist economics and the happenings of revolutionary Russia were obviously a valued part of Wellington's working-class community.

As well as running its Sunday morning economics classes, Josephs was also a speaker at the party's Sunday night lectures, giving talks on "Socialism vs Orthodox Religion," "Martyrs of Modern Times," and "Anarchism and Outrage" during 1906.[16] His lecture on anarchism was reported in Wellington's main paper, the *Evening Post*:

> Mr. P. Josephs delivered an address to a large audience last evening at the Socialist Party's Room, Druids Hall... The speaker gave a sketch of the anarchist philosophy, which, like Socialism, was often misunderstood. He denied that anarchist writers or teachers could be found to advocate violence in any form. He held that all such outrages, even when traced (which was rare) to members of anarchist groups, were the result of economic conditions, and the blame must be placed on society, and not on the individual. A general discussion on anarchism followed.[17]

If Josephs was neither a cloak-and-dagger terrorist as stereotyped by the press, nor an advocate of individual acts of violence, then what did he and his anarchist communist comrades want? And how would they get it? In contrast to bourgeois individualism and its assertion of the right to do anything one pleased, and with a deepening of Bakunin's collectivist position (which held that the means of production should be held in common, but that labour would still be renumerated by the amount performed), anarchist communists such as Josephs believed "genuine freedom and individuality could only exist in a free society." They stressed a new social order based on distribution according to need, the absence of any kind of wage system, and mutual aid.[18] "There is no valid way of measuring the value of any one person's economic contribution," they argued, "because all wealth is a collective product of current and preceding generations."[19] Therefore any measurement of an individual's output would lead to competition and the enforcement of property rights—anathema to anarchist thought. A truly libertarian society, one that balanced individual freedom with collective responsibility, would be one without class, exploitation, exchange, and private property—in other words, free communism. As the handsomely designed header of Josephs' *Maoriland Worker* ads announced, free communism was a voluntary social arrangement based on the principle: from each according to ability, to each according to need.[20]

Social revolution from below, through self-organized class struggle and the collective activity of the workers and peasants, was seen as the means of bringing about an anarchist communist society. In contrast to the state socialists' calls for nationalisation and political reform, and in rejection of orthodox Marxism—whose dictatorship of the proletariat would use and strengthen state power in a transitory period (which would then whither away)—figures like Kropotkin denied the need for any transition period and argued for immediate communism. For Kropotkin, the means used to bring about the revolution must match the ends, and therefore any revolutionary minority taking over state power would simply become a new ruling class. Instead, the abolition of the state and "expropriation of the whole of social wealth" by the people themselves would ensure a "self-managed, socialist, and stateless social order."[21] Josephs shared such a position, and used every available means during his time in New Zealand to propagate it.

Another anarchist communist with connections to the Wellington branch of the NZSP was Dr. Thomas Fauset Macdonald, a visitor to New Zealand in 1906, who knew Kropotkin and the anarchist archivist and historian Max Nettlau, and had ties to the British anarchist movement. Born in Maryhill, Glasgow, Macdonald had graduated from Glasgow University in 1882, where he specialized in tropical diseases. Before his scientific research prompted him to leave his London surgery and embark on an extensive tour of Australasia in the late 1890s, Macdonald was an established public speaker in England, one-time member of Freedom Press (UK), and in 1893 was both the benefactor and ghost editor of the UK *Commonweal* (previously edited by Morris of the Socialist League until it passed hands to the anarchist David Nicoll in 1890).[22] According to Nicoll, Macdonald was "a middle-class gentleman... liberal with money and not unpopular. He was naturally an authority on scientific subjects and understood chemistry."[23]

When he arrived in New Zealand, the London ex-pat "introduced himself to the then Honorary Secretary of the Wellington Branch of the Party as an anarchist communist," and energetically engaged himself in the scene. Macdonald's "clearness of vision" and "honesty of purpose" was put to good use.[24] As well as lecturing on behalf of the Discharged Prisoners' Aid Society, he gave numerous talks on socialism and anarchism, published a number of medical pamphlets and regularly penned articles in the *Commonweal*, such as "Humanist Interpretations of Crime"; "The Prime Minister" (a satirical text mocking those in power); and "Freedom and Union"—"the principles which provide the anarchist-communistic ideal of a freely federated humanity."[25] In late 1906, he toured the country advocating for an Imperial Labour Conference in London, which was warmly approved of in a printed address to Macdonald delivered by "representatives of the labour movement, the Socialist Party, and others interested in the economic advances of the masses." The undersigned recognized "the enormous potentialities of a gathering of Labour representatives," and added, "we believe the seed you have sown amongst us will grow."[26] His activity eventually caught the attention of conservative cartoonist William Blomfield, who put ink to paper in order to ridicule Macdonald.

Yet despite his views on equality and solidarity, there was a far-from-anarchist undertone. Macdonald was a racialist who used his scientific research to promote racial superiority theories. While in Australasia he pioneered the White Australia movement due to his belief in "guarding against military and economic invasions of Eastern peoples whose standards of living are lower than ours." For Macdonald, such an invasion would lead to "the ultimate destruction and death of our race," and to further his views in New Zealand he formed the White Race League in 1907.[27] Numerous press interviews, pamphlets, and letters to Nettlau are rife with discriminate statements that betray his racism. The labour question in the antipodes, wrote Macdonald, faced "the element of cheap, coloured, absolutely servile alien labour... with the presence of Japanese, Chinese and other eastern peoples, the workers of Australia have had an extra battle to fight."[28]

Macdonald's view that white workers should be protected from 'alien labour' was not uncommon in certain sections of the labour movement, but it was a far cry from the internationalist position of the NZSP who, like most anarchists, saw all workers as having shared class interests regardless of colour. Macdonald's defence of the empire was also at odds with anarchist critiques of the nation state.

To make matters worse, it appears the fore-mentioned address commending Macdonald may have been pure fiction. A *Commonweal* editorial states that the NZSP never signed any address and insisted Macdonald wrote it himself. Because of this and his racism, Macdonald soon fell out of favour with the party. In July 1907, he was officially condemned.[29]

By September, Macdonald was back in Liverpool, before leaving again to visit his "old friend" Kropotkin in Paris. Macdonald then intended to return to Britain to "awaken the people, by means of lectures and articles, to the danger which threatens the Empire from the coloured races at Australia's door."[30] It is unclear what Kropotkin thought of Macdonald's racist activities or what affect his lectures had in Britain. In 1910, Macdonald's contradictory politics died with him on a research trip to West Africa. It is likely that a tropical disease was the cause of his demise.

Internationalism, and the notion of one worldwide class of workers in common struggle, was an important part of being a revolutionary. Alongside the international anarchist and socialist movement, the Wellington branch of the NZSP participated in transnational rituals that celebrated the Paris Commune, May Day, and the Haymarket Affair, informally connecting their local actions with comrades abroad. "His Majesty's Theatre" reported the *Evening Post* in 1906, "was well filled last evening on the occasion of the May celebration of the Wellington Socialists simultaneously with the Socialists of the world." As well as sending fraternal greetings to comrades engaged in the universal class war (quoted in the introduction to this book), Josephs spoke in favour of strike action and against the ICA (the legislation outlawing strikes).[31] In December of that year, Josephs also spoke at an NZSP meeting to commemorate the execution of the 'Chicago Martyrs'—four anarchists (as well as a fifth, who in taking his own life denied the US state the pleasure) who were executed for their alleged role in the bombing of policemen during a Chicago demonstration for the eight-hour working day. Macdonald—not yet condemned by the NZSP—was another speaker, who "referred to the US Governmental conspiracy which led to the judicial murder of [Albert] Parsons and his comrades," before proceeding with his prepared speech on the philosophical inheritance of Kropotkin, Bakunin, and others.[32] Again, in November 1907, a meeting of socialists and anarchists commemorated the "political murder of the men who had become known throughout the world as the Chicago martyrs," and heard "from an anarchist standpoint" personal evidence on the conspiracy from future NZSP literary secretary (and party librarian) Thomas Eagle—the speaker "having been associated with some of their comrades."[33]

Mark Derby has uncovered an interesting New Zealand connection to the Haymarket anarchists. During the trial, August Spies, one of the accused, was asked about explosives he admitted possessing while printing a revolutionary circular in the office of the leftwing German-language newspaper, *Arbeiter Zeitung* (Workers' Newspaper):

Q. How many bombs did you have in the office of the *Arbeiter Zeitung*?
A. I think there were four of these shells... and I think two others. They were iron cast, and given to me by a person, I believe his name was Schwape or Schwoep, who left for New Zealand.[34]

According to Spies, this mystery shoemaker from Cleveland "had visited the *Arbeiter Zeitung* office three years previously and then announced his intention to travel to New Zealand." Whether he ever travelled to New Zealand is also a mystery. As Derby notes, "given the vagueness of the details, immigration records of the time cannot confirm his arrival in New Zealand."[35] However, it does highlight the transient nature of labour and the internationalism of the anarchist movement during this period—a transnationalism that, as early as the 1880s, tentatively included New Zealand.

In a sort of nervous comedy, the newspapers of the day were quick to make light of the apparent development of an anarchist movement in New Zealand. "Stop! Look out for the bomb... The anarchists have come; they are in Wellington; they are sharpening up their choppers," wrote the *Evening Post*, while simultaneously reassuring the reader that "last night's anarchists were mostly our old friends, the out-and-out socialists." "Wellington grew uneasy on Tuesday when it read in the morning papers that there had been a meeting of anarchists in their city," mused the *New Zealand Free Lance*. "People looked about their verandas and gas-boxes in livid fear of finding bombs."[36]

The only bombs the citizens of Wellington would have uncovered however, was mental dynamite in the form of anarchist pamphlets and newspapers. For when Bill Sutch in *The Quest for Security in New Zealand* wrote that "tons of pamphlets and books were imported and circulated by the Socialist Party—anarchist pamphlets, IWW (Industrial Workers of the World) literature" and more, he was not exaggerating.[37] Mere months after his arrival in Wellington, Josephs was ordering a steady stream of propaganda from Freedom Press (UK) and other anarchist print shops, which were advertised in local socialist newspapers, such as the *Commonweal* and later, the *Maoriland Worker*, or distributed to subscribers around New Zealand. His tailor-shop-cum-bookshop "specializing in anarchist and socialist literature was a central part of the Wellington scene," and remained so for many years—until the New Zealand government put a stop to his mail-order activities in 1915.[38]

As well as the bookstore's cultural impact on the Wellington milieu, the material imported by Josephs played a major part in the influx of revolutionary international literature around the entire country, and was instrumental in creating informal international anarchist networks between New Zealand and anarchist comrades abroad. As one hostile author in the *Auckland Star* confirmed sourly, the "Americanization of the New Zealand Socialist party has been consummated. Its members have been almost exclusively fed on American pamphlets."[39]

As a forerunner of today's anarchist infoshops, Josephs' tailor shop and bookshop was a working class cultural space where all budding revolutionaries were welcome. Tom Barker, syndicalist and key member of both the New Zealand and Australian IWW, remembers Josephs' shop as a hub for radicals, and recalls meeting a Wobbly called Jones there while on an organizing tour in 1913 (this was probably Joseph Herbert Jones, committee member of the Wellington IWW).[40] Between sewing machines, pulleys, pressing irons and a button-hole machine, workers could converse, browse anarchist pamphlets such as "The Wage System" (Kropotkin), "Talk About Anarchist Communism," (Malatesta) or "Tragedy of Women's Emancipation" (Goldman), and measure up for a custom-made suit.[41] "Having studied the economic condition of the Working Class in New Zealand, we have come to the conclusion that the wages they receive make it impossible for them to live as comfortable and dress as useful Workers ought to live and dress," ran Josephs' ads in the *Commonweal*. "It was our duty to establish... 'The International Clothing Company' here in Wellington, where all Working Men are invited to come and get their Suits and Overcoats—first-class and made to measure."[42] It is likely he dressed most of Wellington's radicals, if not the NZSP!

After measuring up and, without a doubt, a rip-roaring discussion on socialism, anarchism, and the state of the labour movement, literature was on hand to continue the investigation at home. Josephs' imported material from anarchist publishing houses such as Freedom Press played a vital part in the spread of anarchist literature and ideas, forming an international mail order network of penny-pamphlets, newspapers, and books. Co-founded by Charlotte Wilson in 1886 and with the services of Kropotkin, Freedom Press was one of the largest anarchist publishing houses at the turn of the twentieth century (and still operates today). Its paper *Freedom* (with the by-line 'A Journal of Anarchist Communism') became the main English-language anarchist paper in Britain, and thanks to distributors such as Josephs, it reached readers far and wide—including willing takers in Taranaki St.

Exactly when Josephs made the decision to stock and distribute anarchist literature is lost to posterity, but it certainly appears that some of his earliest thoughts in Wellington were to spread the ideas of anarchism in his new home and to help build the anarchist movement in New Zealand. On 3 June 1904—three months after arriving in Wellington—Josephs ordered two parcels of books and sixty pamphlets from Freedom Press, starting a relationship that would continue until 1916. Every couple of months Josephs would fill more and more of his tailor shop with radical material—by 1908 he had ordered over £7 worth of books and *Freedom* newspapers (amounting to over $US600 in today's terms). Considering each pamphlet, and *Freedom* itself, only cost 1 pence each, it is easy to imagine Wellington saturated in copious amounts of anarchist material. Indeed, when compared with other *Freedom* stockists in their account books, Josephs' orders were some of the largest and most regular. He is also the only person from New Zealand on the books at that time.[43]

Those who took home a copy of *Freedom* or one of Josephs' numerous anarchist pamphlets would have received a dose of anarchist doctrine and the advocacy of direct action not previously prevalent in the city. In a booklet stocked by Josephs called "Trade Unionism and Anarchism," Jay Fox describes why anarchists, contrary to popular misconception, involved themselves in unions and the labour movement:

> The Anarchist sees in the growth of the trade union an evidence of the tendency towards the simple, natural, yet scientific state of society he is working for. Man has been robbed and enslaved first by the private ownership of land, and later his robbery was increased by the private ownership of the houses in which he lived, the factories in which he worked, and the tools he used. So the landlord, the banker, and the capitalist rob him by way of rent, interest, and profit... The same condition of mind and intelligence produce the unionist and the Anarchist, who are often one and the same person. In striving to better his lot in the present, he is a unionist; in mapping out a condition of freedom and equality for the future, he is an Anarchist.[44]

Scottish anarchist Guy Aldred's "Logic and Economics of Class Struggle," French anarchist and syndicalist Emile Pouget's "The Basis of Trade Unionism," and other pamphlets in Josephs' possession highlight his interest in the labour movement and a brand of anarchism that, in contrast to the individualism often ascribed to it, put forward class struggle, industrial unionism, and the direct action of the working class.

However, Josephs' road to an anarchist presence in New Zealand was not an easy one. For in 1908 the initial bubble that was four years of sustained anarchist activity burst. In December 1907 Josephs was in the Magistrate's Court due to conflict with one of his employees.

"[Josephs] claimed £20 damages on account of the defendant, whom he had engaged as a machinist, leaving him in the busy season, and putting him to great expense to get another hand. The defendant alleged dismissal as the reason why he left."[45] The defendant was ruled to be at fault and Josephs won his case, but the victory was short lived. In August 1908 he was declared bankrupt.[46]

Either Josephs was bad with money, or a little credulous. After starting his business with a mere £7, "Josephs took in two partners [Heley and Nisbett] with aggregate cash £485," wrote the Evening Post. "Within six months both partners had gone out [at a loss], and a month or two later Josephs filed for his schedule." Josephs admitted that his partners' incoming money was needed to pay off debts and that he had told his second partner Nisbett "the business was a flourishing one." But Josephs argued this was based on "Heley's statement of accounts. Heley was the bookkeeper. According to balance-sheets shown Nisbett, there was a weekly turnover of £90, and after all expenses were met there was a profit of £21 15s to divide. He (Josephs) did not know that such balance sheets were false."[47] Although the court believed Josephs and the account books he provided as evidence to be true, the magistrate noted that a discharge from bankruptcy would encourage "a system of reckless and speculative trading."[48] As a result, a vast amount of tailoring equipment, and the shop itself, was placed in receivership.

Maybe Josephs' love of gambling, or that he was overly generous with his anarchist material (often giving it away for free), was the real cause of his financial woes. Either way, Josephs was now bankrupt, without a shop and with little cash for anarchist literature. His activity ground to a halt. Josephs' adverts in the Commonweal lingered on until April 1908, but apart from one or two brief comments, he practically disappears from the Commonweal and NZSP records from then onwards (although that year the NZSP tightened into a more doctrinal party in the classical Marxist sense that, as an anarchist, may not have sat well with his politics). It would take another two years for Josephs to beat debt's blues and resume his anarchist agitation in earnest.

CHAPTER 5

TO HELL WITH LAW AND AUTHORITY[1]

Around the time of Josephs' financial misfortune, workers across New Zealand were increasingly questioning what was perceived to be a bankrupt system—arbitration. Economic conditions, workers' self-activity of significant proportions, and a procession of international agitators gave rise to a fight between capital and labour that challenged both 'labour's leg iron' and the capitalist system itself. For a brief but tumultuous period, class struggle succeeded in rupturing the mechanisms of arbitration and capitalist domination in New Zealand on a scale that, arguably, has yet to be matched. With this international upsurge of struggle came revolutionary syndicalist organizations and increased anarchist activity in New Zealand, explicitly through anarchist adherents in various parts of the country, or implicitly in the form of the New Zealand IWW. And despite its limited recognition in labour historiography, this anarchist activity certainly played a role during the period. While never creating a mass organization of their own, anarchists were part of the syndicalist current—a storm of activity that placed the ideology of direct action squarely in the sights (and hands) of many workers.

Although the Industrial Conciliation and Arbitration Act (ICA) had encouraged the growth of trade unions in New Zealand, "a complex interplay of changing work patterns, a rapidly expanding workforce and the bankruptcy of traditional union strategies" led to widespread dissatisfaction with the arbitration system.[2] Le Rossignol and Stewart, in *State Socialism in New Zealand*, noted:

> it is not easy to show that compulsory arbitration has greatly benefited the workers of the colony. Sweating has been abolished but it is a question of whether it would not have disappeared in the

years of prosperity without the help of the Arbitration Court. Strikes have largely been prevented, but it is possible that the workers might have gained as much or more by dealing directly with their employers than by the mediation of the court. As to wages, it is generally agreed that they have not increased more than the cost of living.[3]

While rent and food prices soared, real wages declined. On his visit to New Zealand in 1909, American labour relations expert Colonel Weinstock, "expressed his surprise that the advance of wages had not been greater, considering the worldwide increase in wages during the period."[4] To add to the discontent, the Arbitration Court repeatedly ruled that high profits for employers did not justify increasing the wages of workers, even though in 'tough' times for employers the Court was happy to freeze or cut pay packets. As a result, between 1894 and 1910, profits swelled the pockets of employers by a whopping 180 percent.[5] Despairing of the slowness and perceived class bias of the Court, workers began to take matters into their own hands.

The first to challenge arbitration was an illegal strike by sixty-six Auckland tramway workers in 1906 who, against the judgement of their union official, walked out in protest after a number of motor men had been dismissed. After ceasing work for half a day and smashing the company's plate glass windows, management caved.[6] This was followed in 1907 by a strike of slaughtermen—200 of which were fined for their illegal action but who simply refused to pay. These successes turned heads, but the "rebellion burst into the open" in 1908 with a strike won by the Blackball Miners' Union, whose defiance against fines and the authority of the presiding judge openly flouted the Arbitration Court and the ICA itself. "It seemed that the Blackball miners had punched a hole through the prison wall and let in a ray of hope," wrote one historian.[7]

The Blackball strike also gave birth to the syndicalist-inspired, openly radical FOL whose call for unions to de-register from the ICA and emphasis on class struggle, industrial organization, and revolution resulted in a rapid increase of membership and influence. In 1911, the FOL doubled in size (from 6,724 to 13,971 members) and by 1912 it had 43 affiliated unions.[8] When the Great Strike of 1913 erupted, the Federation had around 15,000 members, representing "over 20 percent of the organized workers of New Zealand."[9] The radicalism of the 'Red Feds' also saw them clash with more moderate unions such as the Trades and Labour Councils, who were seen by the FOL as craft-orientated, divisive, and too conciliatory with both employers and the state. Ironically, it was not long before the New Zealand IWW charged the FOL with the exact same faults.

It was the bold actions of the tramway workers, Blackball miners, and the FOL that helped to ignite a bitter struggle between capital and labour—a struggle that included the first recorded death of a worker in an industrial dispute (during the 1912 Waihi Strike) and, in the minds of more optimistic radicals, reached the cliffs of revolutionary change during the Great Strike of 1913. Recorded industrial disputes rose from zero in 1905 to seventy-three in 1913, while the visits of international agitators, such as Tom Mann (1902, 1908), Harry Fitzgerald (1907–1910, 1912), John Benjamin King (1911–1912), and numerous others, added fuel to the flames, bringing "influences into New Zealand that reflected the contemporaneous international increase in socialist activity."[10] Their skills as orators ensured that exposés of capitalist exploitation and the straightjacket of arbitration fell on eager ears.

Interestingly, Josephs had penned a lengthy article in the January 1907 edition of *Commonweal* titled "Trades Unionism in New Zealand: Is it a Failure?" that strongly denounced arbitration and advocated strike action a full year before such a stance would be made popular by Fitzgerald, FOL co-founder Patrick Hickey, and other syndicalists.

As well as giving a brief history of the development of trade unionism in general ("a tremendous struggle to wring from their exploiters the right of combination") and an analysis of the 1890 Maritime Strike (which failed due to the intervention of political interests and "the want of organization"), Josephs lambasted the "reactionary, disorganized, and almost non-existent" model of craft unionism in New Zealand, arguing that the working class had been dealt "its death blow" by being "robbed of their fighting weapon, the Strike." Instead, "the exploiter and the exploited meet and mutually arrange the amount of exploitation which satisfied the rapaciousness of the former,"wrote Josephs in disbelief. As a result, union officials had "lost sight of the true principle on which their organizations were based," and "instead of union standing by union, we find them often fighting each other at the behest of their leaders and, we may be sure, to the advantage of their employers."[11] His critique of craft unionism, the corrupting influences of centralisation and power, and the advocacy of strike action represent both an anarchist viewpoint and an accurate reading of the mood of the day.

Despite Josephs' temporary taciturnity after his article was published, anarchist activity across the country was increasingly visible during this period—carried on the crest of class struggle and the influx of radical propaganda. In 1907, Greymouth's *Grey River Argus* republished French anarchist Ernest Lesigne's well-known *Le Radical* letter, "Socialism and Anarchism," which portrayed anarchism in a positive light:

There are two Socialisms...
One wishes all monopolies to be held by the State;
the other wishes the abolition of all monopolies.
One wishes the governed class to become the governing class;
the other wishes the disappearance of classes...

One says:
The land to the State.
The mine to the State.
The tool to the State.
The product to the State.

The other says:
The land to the cultivator.
The mine to the miner.
The tool to the labourer.
The product to the producer.[12]

A more concrete example of anarchist influence on the West Coast is the part Fay McMasters played in a wildcat strike by Otira Tunnel workers in 1908. Since construction began on the 8.5 kilometre tunnel in 1907, arduous and wet work had contributed to strained relations between workers and management. As a result, Otira was a site of constant spontaneous strikes and union organizing—the perfect environment for overtures of anarchist oration. In his diary entry of 12 June, Fabian socialist and president of the Canterbury Trades and Labour

Council, Jack McCullough, states that the presence of socialist newspapers such as *The Clarion* in Otira was due to McMasters—a former soldier in the Black Watch (an infantry battalion of the Scottish Royal Highlanders) and self-described anarchist communist. Before ending up in Otira, McMasters had given "a very interesting lecture on 'The Labour Movement At Home'" to listeners in Wellington, had briefly joined the literary staff of the *Commonweal*, and had penned the odd book review.[13] "He is a remarkably well read man" testified an Otira-confined McCullough: "in the evenings from 9 to 10.30 he held forth in the smoking room for the instruction of all who cared to listen."[14] A month later Otira workers were on strike—without the blessing of union officials.[15]

New Zealand had another European emigrant during this period. In 1906, Johann Sebastian Trunk—German cabinetmaker, militant anarchist, and advocate of propaganda by the deed—migrated with his wife and daughter to Christchurch to work with his brother-in-law at Lutjohann & Co., a producer of billiard tables. Trunk had been a key part of the London anarchist milieu as editor of Johann Most's fiery paper *Freiheit* (Freedom) while Most was in prison, and was both organizer of and delegate to the 1881 London Social Revolutionary Congress "as a representative of Der Kommunistischer Arbeiterbildungsverein [Communist Workers' Educational Association], a German-speaking workers' association that included socialists, anarchists and other revolutionaries." He also spoke from the soapbox alongside Lucy Parsons during her visit to London in 1888.[16] Trunk was naturalized in October 1908 and forced to register as an alien in 1917, yet little more is known about this revolutionary's activity in the antipodes. The most concrete record of his time in New Zealand is a headstone in the rural town of Geraldine that notes his death on 4 June 1933, age eighty-two.

As well as foreign activists, the availability of anarchist literature was on the rise in the South Island. McCullough noted in a 1909 diary entry that he bought a book "on Anarchy" after a round of browsing in Christchurch, while the local Rationalist Association (headed by free-thinking MP William Collins) published *Ferrer And His Enemies*, illustrating that anarchist or related material was readily available in the city.[17] Indeed, the great majority of socialist literature in New Zealand at that time was anarchist or revolutionary syndicalist: "what little Marxist literature that was available was swamped" by that of anarchism and the IWW.[18]

In New Zealand's northern-most newsstands, anarchism found a sympathetic avenue in the form of the *Social Democrat*, the lively newspaper of the Auckland branch of the NZSP. The branch's swing towards revolutionary syndicalism was reflected in its paper, and ensured that its publishing of Goldman and Kropotkin quotes was not out of place. In fact, the paper—thanks to its editor, the Australian revolutionary socialist Harry Scott Bennett—actively conferred credibility to the anarchist position. In March 1912, Bennett noted excitedly that "a debate on Direct Action vs. Political Action between Emma Goldman, the world's most famous and greatest anarchist, and Sol Fieldman, Socialist lecturer and orator" was soon to take place in New York; while a front page passage in April satirically slammed the fact-less sensationalism of the mainstream press:

> Anarchism! What an awful word! And yet such a word supplies the capitalist editors with a subject for readers. *The Herald*, for instance, tells us that 'the anarchist doctrine has only existed since 1872,' and proceeds by naming Bakunin as its founder. Of course, its too much to expect the capitalist editors to state that Max Stirner in his book *Der Einzige und sein Eigentum* [The Ego and Its Own], was the first to promote the doctrine of anarchism in the year 1845, and that three years later Proudhon also added his quotes to the same philosophy.[19]

In another editorial quip, the *Democrat* lamented the fact "the anarchist bogey [had] made its appearance in Auckland. The irony of it! All those who do not kow-tow to wowserism, opportunism, and worse, are anarchists!"[20] However Bennett knew better. Anarchist communism, "as expressed by Prince Kropotkin and Malatesta," was not the same as the "calumny and crime hurled at the modern anarchist movement," went his lecture 'Anarchy plus the Policeman' to a packed hall in Auckland. Instead, it was "the secret police of different countries" that created sensation "for political purposes and the crushing of militant proletarian organizations."[21]

Readers of the *Social Democrat* were informed of Christchurch events thanks to the updates of Wyatt E. Jones, whose adverts in the *Maoriland Worker* carried the byline: "Watchmaker and anarchist... Exploitation at a Minimum."[22] Like Josephs, Jones was a member of the NZSP and a regular speaker from the soapbox. In July 1911, he received a fine of

10s and costs for denouncing capitalism in Christchurch's Cathedral Square. He did not seem to have been deterred however, for he never turned up to court, and according to the *Ashburton Guardian* he later chaired a meeting of unemployed in the Square where he urged that government work only be accepted for at least £2 a week. The motion passed without dissent.[23]

Jones was also apt with the pen. In October 1912, the *Maoriland Worker* republished a letter from Jones to Magistrate Francis Frazer, who had just jailed twenty-three participants in a long-running strike at the massive Waihi goldmine. According to Jones, Frazer was "a puppet in the hands of relentless greed" who, instead of simply interpreting the law, had abused his role "like many another with too much power." He concluded ominously: "Sir, take warning, as the day is not far distant when you and the class you represent will be shown their real place in the great scheme of the economic revolution."[24]

The influence of anarchism in Christchurch is further illustrated by incidents involving local adherents who, in the prevailing atmosphere of direct action politics, were finally breaking free of the NZSP. In 1910, the city's branch had no money in its social and general accounts, while the literature committee, which operated on a separate fund, had full coffers. Needing money for an upcoming election campaign, a motion was passed to join the three accounts together:

> Unfortunately for this scheme the membership of the literature committee were anarchist to a man, and had no use for elections… Immediately the meeting concluded the literature committee went to work. By the small hours of the following morning they had completed their labours, which consisted of the ordering of over £100 worth of pamphlets and booklets… when they had finished, their finances were in the same state as the rest of the branch.[25]

Unsurprisingly, at the following meeting the resignation of the literature committee was called for. The anarchists in question cheerfully left the party and promptly formed themselves into a branch of the IWW, receiving their charter from the US IWW in March 1912.[26] Among them was Syd Kingsford, future agent of Josephs' mailbox movement.[27]

Tensions within the branch did not end there, however. Factions flared again in January 1912 when Jones (who had remained in the party) and a member named Jamieson were accused of disloyalty for "repeatedly ridiculing Parliamentary Action" in public. A motion was moved that declared: "all anarchist communists should be asked for their resignation, failing this, to be expelled... Anarchist communists were anti-socialist and must be in the Party to destroy it."[28] At his 'trial' and amid constant interruptions, Jones spoke for forty-five minutes, defending the cause of direct action, his placement of "principles before vote-catching, and the economic education of the people in the class war before attempting to win a seat in Parliament." Despite the presence of W. Tusker, a NZSP member who stated during a lecture called 'Socialism versus Anarchy' that he "would join the Capitalist ranks and shoot down anarchists, anarchist communists and 'cuckoos,'" the trial ended in deadlock—members were divided (some even left the room in protest at having to vote) and the quorum needed for expulsion was not met.[29] Reporting on the incident, the *Social Democrat* took sides with Jones and Jamieson, noting that the Christchurch branch had refused to "push the sale of the SOCIAL DEMOCRAT as it speaks the truth [of revolutionary syndicalism] too plainly." "Members of the Branch might be better with a dose of medicine," it added slyly.[30]

Jones' 'Open Letter to the New Zealand Socialist Party' in the *Social Democrat* describes the debate:

We Revolutionary Socialists of Christchurch have a message for you. 'Our Comrades,' we are despoiled of our just heritage, debarred from the Socialist Party, and the reason is—because we are Revolutionary Socialists. For eighteen months I have remained in the Christchurch Socialist Party to fight for the cause of 'Revolutionary Industrial Socialism,' or IWWism. Time and time again I have been told by its members and self-constituted leaders that my place was outside, that the 'Socialist Party' was peculiarly a 'political party,' and no place to propagate IWWism. Sydney Kingsford, Stanley Roscoe, J. Woods, C. Shepherd, W. Griffiths and other comrades were forced out of this party many months ago on similar grounds... their fault was that they were students, and wanted 'Socialism' by the best methods.[31]

According to Jones, parliamentary politics—"Petit Bourgeois in thought and action"—were products of "an antiquated period" to which the

Christchurch branch clung "in fear of offending the bosses." "If I am disloyal to such a party," concluded Jones, "then I am proud of my disloyalty… I join with my other revolutionary comrades outside,recognising that this party is no place for us."[32]

Another anarchist communist who resigned from the Christchurch branch in protest was Len Wilson, prominent member of the Canterbury Farm Labourer's Union and one of the branch's oldest members. Wilson had joined the party in 1904, was the financial secretary throughout 1907 and 1908, and during the Blackball strike had scoured the streets collecting money for the strike fund. Like Jones, he often soapboxed in Cathedral Square. In May 1908, Wilson riveted an enormous crowd with an anarchist attack on the medical fraternity, and according to the *Commonweal*, he frequently and "nobly" debated with hecklers and anti-socialist speakers.[33] Mrs. Wilson (Len's wife) was also a member of the branch, juggling her position on the executive committee with her role as president of the Domestic Workers' Union.[34] Whether she shared his anarchist politics is unknown, but in a letter to the *Social Democrat*, Len made his own position crystal clear:

I read in this week's DEMOCRAT that I have resigned from the Christchurch Branch of the Socialist Party, because of being a communist anarchist. This is true, but I wish it to be plainly understood that I personally have no quarrel with the individual members of the above Branch. For eight years I have worked side by side with Comrade Cooke [then-secretary of the branch] and others for the cause, and it is no pleasant task to have to pull out from the fight, but seeing that my opinions have changed and I do not now believe in the worker receiving the full product of his labour [in the collectivist sense], nor in the soundness of majority rule, I could not consistently and honourably remain an active member of a party that makes these two planks part of its platform… Yours for freedom and justice, LEN R. WILSON.[35]

Having declared "himself a communist anarchist" wrote the *Democrat*, and clashing with the party's view "about Socialism being a State society under democratic government, etc… Len got out."[36]

Despite his leaving, Wilson resumed his anarchist activity and continued to preach socialism from the sidewalk. By all accounts, he was a lively speaker. "Our comrade can quote scripture," wrote the *Maoriland Worker* about his speech to a large Cathedral Square crowd: "Suffer little children to come unto me, and I will sweat their blooming hearts out," preached a satirical Wilson in the voice of "our capitalistic friend."[37] It seems he was too lively for some. Speaking outside one of the NZSP's well attended 'Sunday Services,' Wilson managed to get "the sailors' backs up. Ten Sons-of-the-Sea-all-British-born wanted to chew Len's lug because Len suggested they were fools to do the protecting business for 1s. 10d. per day."[38] The city's police also did not take kindly to Wilson's public performances; in April 1913, he was prosecuted for speaking sense from the steps of Christchurch's clock tower.[39]

The party's loss was the IWW's gain. The radicals around the country who rejected the 'petit bourgeois' politics of the NZSP found a more accommodating home amongst the direct actionists of the IWW—and for good reason. After its 1905 founding in the United States, the IWW was a revolutionary syndicalist organization that won the support of workers around the world. As well as being open to workers of any gender or colour, the IWW was popular for promoting the idea of the 'One Big Union,' a fighting union that—through the solidarity of all workers organized along class lines instead of trade, and the use of the general strike—would abolish capitalism and the wage system. However, it was much more than a simple union movement. Its fostering of a working-class counter-culture, through their hugely influential use of song, poetry, and graphics, made it a social and cultural movement on an international scale.

In his study of the New Zealand IWW, Stuart Moriarty-Patten writes that the IWW successfully "provided an explanation and proposed a solution for the problems faced by the working class that was grounded in the everyday life experiences of their audience"; solutions that resonated with New Zealand workers.[40] In December 1907, New Zealand's first IWW local was formed in Wellington, and as we have seen, other locals quickly formed in Christchurch and Auckland (which in 1912 also received its charter from IWW headquarters in Chicago, becoming Local 175).[41] Informal groups sprung up in industrial towns such as Huntly, Waihi, and Denniston, and the cultural norms and tactics championed by the Wobblies—such as the general strike, sabotage, and the go-slow (working at speeds harmful to production and the bosses' pockets)— soon spiced the local discourse of struggle. The rally-cry of 'a fair day's wage' was dropped for 'abolish the wage system;' 'fellow-worker' (the term Wobblies used to address each other in America) quickly replaced 'comrade'; and for a period, the FOL even adopted the IWW's revolutionary preamble.[42] Looking back on his time in New Zealand, Tom Barker claimed the IWW's advocacy of the go-slow was so successful that between 1908 and 1913, employers were complaining about a 15 percent drop in production speed—a nightmare for any boss.[43]

The relationship between anarchism and the IWW is the topic of much historiography—ranging from the view that anarchism was a major, if not the primary driver of the IWW's tactics and ideas (via revolutionary syndicalism), to the notion that the IWW was more Marxist than syndicalist, and that it developed independently and separately to syndicalism.[44] It is clear that, from its formation, the New Zealand IWW had a number of anarchist members and sympathisers, attracted to its promotion of rank-and-file control, workers' self-activity and direct action; and its relentless critique of leaders, union bureaucracy, and the state. Anarchists and the IWW shared the space to the left of the FOL, which was criticized for its involvement in parliamentary politics, its centralized executive, and lack of industrial organization. According to Erik Olssen in *The Red Feds*, "in Auckland if not elsewhere, Wobblies, socialists, industrial unionists and even the occasional anarchist co-operated on day-to-day tasks."[45]

Nonetheless, evidence of the New Zealand IWW's actual stance on anarchism is limited. The only article specifically addressing anarchism in the *Industrial Unionist* (the newspaper of the New Zealand IWW) conflates individualist anarchism with the anarchist communism of activists like Josephs, Jones, and Wilson, and seemingly distances itself from it—arguing "the anarchist is more idealist than materialist... anarchism is not a class movement."[46] In a sense they were right—a number of anarchists did view all morally and spiritually oppressed people as revolutionary agents, rather than the working class as a class. Yet an editorial on the very same page announces their pride in being associated with "extremists" and "such fearsome terms as SYNDICALISM, REVOLUTIONARY UNIONISM, ANARCHISM etc."[47] In a later issue, a lively article titled "Law and Order," by popular Wobbly orator Harry Melrose, made it clear that "the necessity for law arose with the inauguration of slavery, and the institution of private property." It ended in defiantly anarchist terms: "Liberty for All—to Hell with Law and Authority!"[48]

The New Zealand IWW's model of a decentralized, rank-and-file organization and the critique of centralized leadership, also drew strongly on anarchist principles. "The IWW considered a reliance on leadership as fostering dependence amongst the working class," notes Moriarty-Patten. "It proves to be inflexible, and often there is a danger of a movement being tied to one symbolic leader."[49] The rotation of responsibilities and the minimization of centralization would "not only prevent the development of a leadership circle, but it would also have the benefit of giving the rank and file workers more experience of decision making, something crucial to developing the confidence of all members of the Union."[50] Writing in the *Industrial Unionist*, one Wobbly decried the fact that "the labour movement is cursed and hampered today by leaders," and argued that "active, intelligent workers in the labour movement [should] determine to do their own thinking... to fight on all occasions for complete control by the rank and file and against sheep-like following of leaders."[51] Echoing the core principles of anarcho-syndicalism, the article continues: "officers must not direct, they must be directed; an executive should be an executive, and nothing more; they should be made to obey instructions or get out."[52] Intentionally or not, the New Zealand IWW was the closest thing to an anarchist labour organization in the country.

The mainstream press certainly believed the IWW were as vile and dangerous as the anarchists, and spared no space in its condemnation of the organization. As the *Industrial Unionist* pointed out, the terms 'IWW' and 'anarchist' were often lumped together—seen simply as one and the same. "Anarchist doctrines," bellowed the *Evening Post*, are "published by an IWW organ in Auckland... No God and no Government is their motto. Their principles... a claim to the right of living without working and killing without fighting."[53] In Waihi, "gallant workers" were fighting the "devilish doctrine" of anarchism and the IWW, who were terrorizing arbitrationists into abandoning "peaceful methods of social reform for strikes, violence, and sabotage."[54]

Some sections of the labour movement also lent their voice to the attack. In distancing the United Federation of Labour (UFL, which replaced the FOL in 1913) from the IWW, future Prime Minister Peter Fraser wrote that the *Industrial Unionist* was "hum-drum" and that anarchism was "too Utopian to be a danger to Capitalism."[55] More moderate officials went further. Mark Fagan, secretary-treasurer of the UFL, argued that anyone who preached "sabotage, anarchy, and syndical-ism... should have their heads chopped off;"[56] while an Auckland news-paper, the *Voice of Labour*, mourned the fact that "anarcho-syndicalism had finally taken root" in New Zealand.[57]

Although Olssen writes "in the last months of 1911 an anarcho-syn-dicalist faction emerged in Auckland," and despite the *Social Democrat's* sympathy to anarchism, he doubts whether they were actually anarcho-syndicalists—arguing that ideological alignments were often born of tactical opportunism.[58] But in a letter to Bert Roth, Auckland Wobbly Alec Holdsworth states there was "an anarchist group in Auckland, who handled syndicalist literature and anti-parliamentarian stuff, with which we had some affinity."[59] In February 1913, one newspaper re-ported in disgust that "No God, No Master" posters could be found pasted around the city.[60] If so, this group pre-dates the Wellington Freedom Group and can claim the title of New Zealand's first anarchist collective. It also shows that anarchists in New Zealand, alongside their comrades in the wider syndicalist movement, were getting organized. Thanks to their efforts, anarchism in New Zealand became more than just a reporter's rouse.

ANARCHY!

WHAT IS IT?

The LEICESTER ANARCHIST-COMMUNISTS
will hold an

OPEN-AIR MEETING

IN

HUMBERSTONE GATE,

On WEDNESDAY, July 18, 1894,

AT 8 P.M.

Dr. FAUSET MACDONALD

Of London,

Will deliver an ADDRESS on

"THE ANARCHISTS' PLAN
OF CAMPAIGN."

QUESTIONS & DISCUSSION INVITED.

Leicester Co-operative Printing Society Ltd., Vauxhall Street, Causeway Lane.

Poster advertsing a talk by Dr Thomas Fauset Macdonald in England, 1894.

ANARCHISM:

ITS ORIGIN AND AIM.

A LECTURE

DELIVERED IN WELLINGTON BY

J. B. FINDLAY, LL.D.

DUNEDIN:
Printed at the Evening Star Job Printing Works, Bond Street
—
1894.

A young Philip Josephs, taken in Glasgow sometime before 1903.

A photograph of Sophia Josephs, taken during the same session.

Wellington's working class dwellings: washing hanging in Te Aro, c. 1910.

THE COMMONWEAL

ORGAN OF THE N.Z. SOCIALIST PARTY.

VOL. I, No. 8.—NEW SERIES.]   WELLINGTON, N.Z., MAY, 1907.   [ONE PENNY

This day are the Workers in every land
Gathered together like one mighty band,
Hear ye their tramp as they march along,
Moved by one impulse, singing one song—
    Vive Proletaire!
      Away with despair,
  Rouse ye, join in the throng.

Now, let our hearts be glad this May morn
A new year of hope for Labour is born;
Cheer for the time when Justice shall reign,
And nations be linked in Fraternity's chain—
    Vive Proletaire!
      Away with despair,
  Comrades rejoice, for we fight not in vain.

          —HACO.

SOCIAL REVOLUTION.

ABOVE: "'I am so sure of a social revolution,' said Dr Macdonald, the Australian Socialist. 'that I don't bother about life insurance, or about banking any money to provide for my family for the future, because I am convinced that a great social revolution is coming.' Supposing the tide rises instead of the rock! What then?" Cartoon by William Blomfield, 1907.

OPPOSITE TOP: Freedom Group member Charles Mumme with three of his sons, c. 1910.

OPPOSITE BOTTOM: Delegates to the fourth annual conference of the NZSP, Dunedin, 1911. Standing in the back row is Charles Mumme (second from left), and Thomas Eagle (second from right).

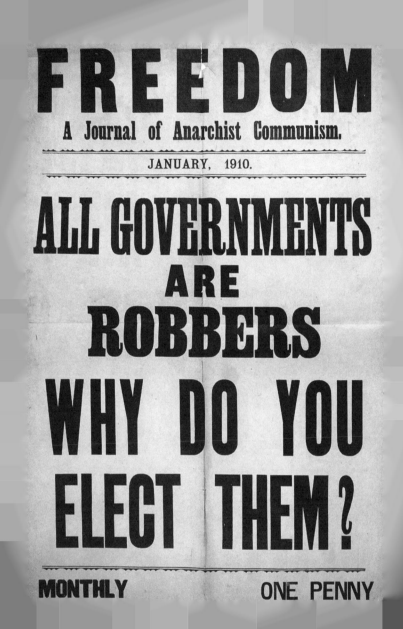

Freierman's Book Store, 12 Ontario Street E., Montreal, Canada

John Chiara, Box 714, Kellogg, Idaho, U.S.A. ——

H. Glasse, 23 Park Lane, Port Elizabeth, Cape Colony ——

P. Josephs, Box 48 G.P.O., Wellington, New Zealand

"Mother Earth," 74 W. 119 St. Street, New York City, U.S.A.

M. Maisel, 422 Grand Street, New York City, U.S.

J. Pope, 5 Foveaux Street, Surrey Hills, Sydney, N.S.W.

W. Nagorooe, 128 S. Eden Street, Baltimore, Md., U.S.

Fritz Ratz, Post Office, Broken Hill South, via Adelaide, South Austra

Feb.	March	April	May	June	July	Aug.	Sept.	Oct.	Nov.	Dec
6	6	6	6	6	6 ✓	6	6	6	6	6
x	x	x	x	x	x	x	x	x	25	25
6	6	6	6	6	6 ✓	6	6	6	6	6
36	36	60	60	60	60	60	60	60	60	60 ✓
		4 posters	4p.	4p.	4p.	4p.	4p.	4p.		4p.
x	x	x	x	x	x	x	x	6	6	6
13	13	13	13	13	13 ✓	13	13	13	13	13
x	x	x	x	x	x	25	25	25	25	25 ✓
5	5	X								
24	24	24	X	12 May 12 June	24 ✓	24	24	24	24	24 ✓

Mounted specials turn and charge at strikers during the Battle of Featherston St, 5 November 1913.

THE NEW ZEALAND
OBSERVER

AN ILLUSTRATED JOURNAL OF INTERESTING AND AMUSING LITERATURE.

Smart, but not vulgar; fearless, but not offensive; independent, but nor neutral; unsectarian, but not irreligious.

ESTABLISHED 1880.

Vol. XXXVII—No 15.] SATURDAY, DECEMBER 16, 1916. [Threepence

THE NOXIOUS WEED. ROOT IT OUT.

New Zealand.

POLICE DEPARTMENT

POLICE DEPARTMENT
15/1465
WELLINGTON, N.Z.

NEW ZEALAND POLICE
20 OCT. 1915
COMMISSIONER'S OFFICE, WELLINGTON

Received: _____ 191

From _____ Solicitor General,
Wellington

Subject :

Philip Josephs, Wellington, distributor
of anarchist literature : censorship of
correspondence advised.

MEMORANDA.

Colonel Gibbon.

Please see attached memorandum from the Solicitor-General.
Will you please instruct the Censor to have all postal matter
for Josephs examined and any anarchist or I.W.W. literature or
correspondence in connection therewith referred to the Solicitor-
General.

Enquiries are being made regarding "Syd. Kingsford, of 136,
Tuam Street, Christchurch," and in the meantime it would probably
be well to have his correspondence censored also.

CW Hendrey.
Inspector,
for Commissioner of Police.
21/10/15.

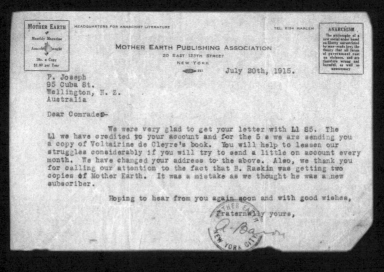

MOTHER EARTH

HEADQUARTERS FOR ANARCHIST LITERATURE

TEL. 6194 HARLEM

ANARCHISM

The philosophy of a new social order based on liberty unrestricted by man-made law; the theory that all forms of government rest on violence, and are therefore wrong and harmful, as well as unnecessary

Monthly Magazine
Anarchist Thought
10c. a Copy
$1.00 per Year

MOTHER EARTH PUBLISHING ASSOCIATION
20 EAST 125TH STREET
NEW YORK

July 20th, 1915.

P. Joseph
95 Cuba St.
Wellington, N. Z.
Australia

Dear Comrades—

We were very glad to get your letter with L1 S5. The L1 we have credited to your account and for the 5 s we are sending you a copy of Voltairine de Cleyre's book. You will help to lessen our struggles considerably if you will try to send a little on account every month. We have changed your address to the above. Also, we thank you for calling our attention to the fact that B. Raskin was getting two copies of Mother Earth. It was a mistake as we thought he was a new subscriber.

Hoping to hear from you again soon and with good wishes,

Fraternally yours,

TOP: Detained letter from Josephs to Emma Goldman, 1915.
ABOVE: Detained letter to Josephs from the Mother Earth Publishing Association, 30 July 1915.

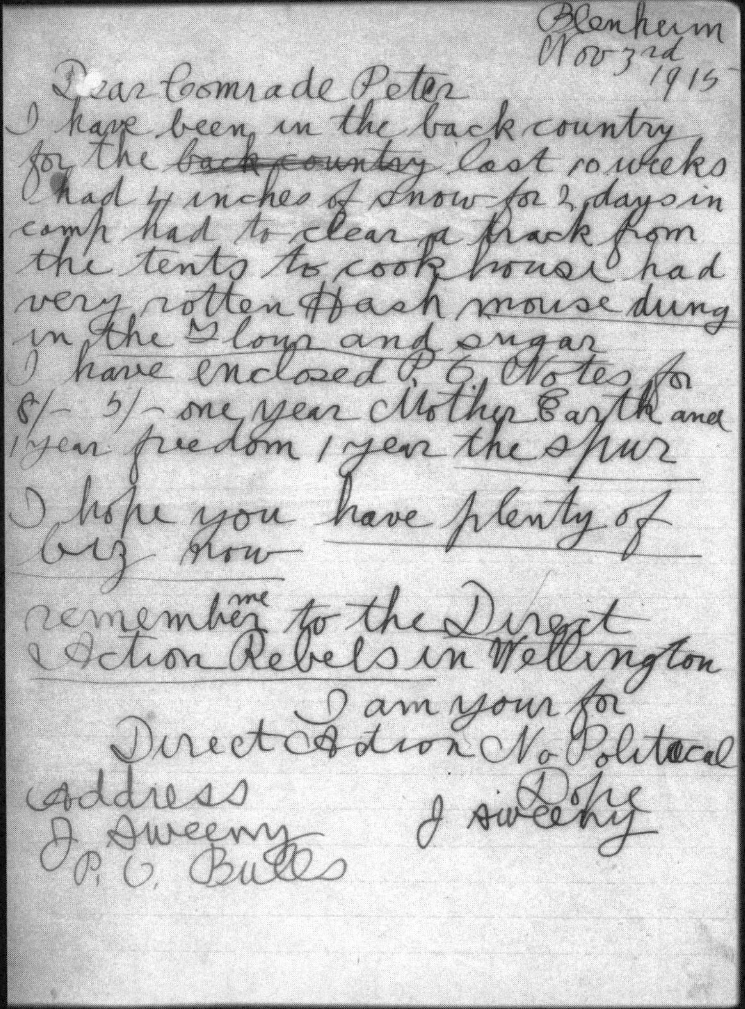

Blenheim
Nov 3rd
1915

Dear Comrade Peter
I have been in the back country
for the ~~back country~~ last 10 weeks
had 4 inches of snow for 2 days in
camp had to clear a track from
the tents to cook house had
very rotten Hash mouse dung
in the Flour and sugar
I have enclosed P. O. Notes for
8/- 5/- one year Mother Earth and
1 year freedom 1 year the spur

I hope you have plenty of
biz now

remember me to the Direct
Action Rebels in Wellington

I am your for
Direct Action No Political
address
J. Sweeny   J Sweeny
P. O. Bull

Letter to Josephs from J Sweeny, 3 November 1915. It never reached its destination.

Sophia Josephs with her youngest daughter Edie, c. 1920.

Philip Josephs in Australia, 1942, age 65.

CHAPTER 6

AN AGENT OF FREEDOM

While the restructuring of capital and its resulting economic conditions contributed to the upsurge of labour militancy, imported literature and the visits of international agitators obviously played vital role in the rise of anarchism and revolutionary syndicalism in New Zealand. Whether from the soapbox or through the pages of socialist newspapers, the transnational diffusion of ideas and tactics captured the heightened class feelings of the day, fostered a sense of solidarity between workers, and helped create counter-institutional formations in New Zealand—a radical counter-culture that informed the mood and methods of militancy. We have already seen the availability of anarchist literature in the country and the scale of Josephs' literary liveliness in the 1904–1908 period, however, after beating bankruptcy in 1910, his later distribution of literature makes his earlier work look like mere child's play. Indeed, in the period leading up to and during the First World War, Josephs had perfected his work. At its peak, he had numerous subscribers and distribution agents of his own up and down the country, and was ordering pamphlets at a rate of sixty per month.

"Dear Comrade. It is quite a while since you heard from me," wrote Josephs in a May 1910 letter to Thomas Keel, then-editor of *Freedom*. "The reason is because I have not been too well off for a considerable time, but am getting better now."[1] Indeed, after a spell of relative silence Josephs seemed back on track. He and the family had moved out of central Wellington to the cheaper rates of Johnsonville (a suburb about seven kilometres north of the city centre). Josephs was working again in Willis Street, and according to court records, was officially discharged from the bounds of bankruptcy on 26 February 1912.[2] He was also re-ordering anarchist literature and drumming up *Freedom* subscribers in the process:

For the last two years I have been distributing the *Freedom* free because I have moved out of town, and buyers in a small village are very scarce, especially for an anarchist paper... it may in time bear some fruit. I received 2/- from [J Kirk of Petone] for a year's subs. for *Freedom*, postage paid.[3]

Josephs also had a wider distribution than Wellington in mind. "I intend to post *Freedom* to various individuals whom I think will be interested in it... it will cost me a little, but it doesn't matter, it is all in the days work." As we shall see, this labour of love would pay dividends in the coming years.

Josephs' personal correspondence with offshore anarchists such as Keel, and the distribution of imported literature kept him (and those interested) in step with the wider anarchist movement, ensuring Josephs was at the forefront of both a transnational sharing of opinions and ideas, and the pulse of revolutionary progress. "The economic struggle was worldwide," confirmed Josephs in the *Commonweal*.[4] As well as Keel, Josephs regularly corresponded with Goldman, Nettlau, and probably a number of others (such was the nature of informal anarchist networks at the time). Having "been in close communication with Emma Goldman for several years," it was Josephs who notified local workers of Goldman's planned lecture tour of Australia and New Zealand in 1909. It was also Josephs who lamented her detention by US authorities, preventing the visit to New Zealand of "one of the most dangerous women in America."[5] He later defended Goldman in a letter to the *Social Democrat*, refuting "the charges made against Emma Goldman in a recent number of *Justice* [a social democratic paper based in the UK]."[6] In another example of global going-ons, a "Note to Correspondents" in the *Maoriland Worker* politely informed Josephs: "the question in dispute is between 'Justice' and 'Freedom,' and there is no reason why we should reprint one side more than the other... sorry can't oblige."[7]

Despite declining to publish Josephs' letter, the early editors of the *Maoriland Worker* were generally sympathetic to anarchism, even if they "did not accept the anarchist line."[8] Numerous columns were dedicated to coverage of international anarchists and the movement's calendar events, such as a faithful biography of Malatesta, and memorials that marked the execution of anarchist educationalist Francisco Ferrer (whose "trial was a farce" according to the paper).[9] The editors also made it clear to their readers that "in literature we are non-doctrinal."[10]

As a result, workers interested in anarchism could purchase Kropotkin's *Fields, Factories and Workshops* and Goldman's *Anarchism* from the *Maoriland Worker*, and from time to time the paper carried favourable reviews of anarchist books such as Frank Harris' *The Bomb* (a novel on the Haymarket Affair) and Kropotkin's landmark text, *The Conquest of Bread*.[11]

Reviews of Goldman's *Anarchism* noted, "this book expresses the most advanced ideas on social questions... it will help the public to understand a group of serious-minded and morally strenuous individuals, and also feel the spirit that underlies the most radical tendencies of the great labour movement today." And in a later issue: "we have frequently mentioned *Anarchism* as thought compelling and meat for strong men and women."[12] In his analysis of Alexander Berkman's *Prison Memoirs of an Anarchist*, Bob Ross waxed poetically: "Alexander Berkman's extraordinary auto-biography... I have read it, only to be torn and tossed, made savage, made humble; baffled, confused, wounded, disgusted, enraged... that this volume is an extraordinary one no critic, however dulled or skilled, may dispute."[13] As late as 1914, the paper was publishing positive reviews of Kropotkin's *Modern Science and Anarchism*, which contained advice "worthy of being borne in mind by every worker in the socialist movement."[14]

Many of the reviews ended with a note advising readers to procure copies from Josephs, and outside of the reviews column the paper also helped raise awareness to this fact. "Michael Bakunin's 'God and the State' is a book 'Canadian Orator Fitzgerald' does not care to be without," ran the *Worker's* endorsement of one of anarchism's seminal texts. "P. Josephs advertises a stock at 6d per copy."[15] And although the *Maoriland Worker* equally published critiques of anarchist ideas and tactics, the sympathy it showed to Josephs and his literature suggests a personal working relationship that helped his cause. Indeed, when Josephs moved his tailor shop to Willis Street, the *Worker* published nothing but praise:

> Mr. P. Josephs, known as literature pusher for anarchism and a trusted lover of the cause... is an expert tailor, and can suit men and execute costumes for women. His ad. appears in this issue, and he deservedly invites patronage.[16]

This solidarity between Josephs and the *Maoriland Worker* was also beneficial to the paper, for as well as providing books and pamphlets to review, Josephs was their primary source for other propaganda. "The Editor of 'Maoriland Worker' wanted I should get 2 doz. Chicago Martyrs," wrote Josephs to Keel in August 1911. "He is going to write a special article on the subject... there will also be a meeting on the 11th Nov. re Chicago Affair, so post them as soon as you get my letter and address it via San Francisco."[17] Sure enough, on 10 November readers awoke to a two-page spread titled 'The Chicago Martyrs: The Men and Their Message,' and photographic portraits of the anarchists in question.[18] With some irony, Josephs repeated the transaction in 1912. "By arrangement with Mr. P. Josephs" wrote the *Worker*, "we are able to offer to the first 30 applicants Prince Peter Kropotkin's great book, 'Mutual Aid,' at 3s per copy."[19]

Josephs' position in Wellington's socialist milieu and his professed anarchist politics ("as far as I know I am the only anarchist in NZ who is not frightened to publicly distribute our literature") secured his place as the most prominent anarchist in New Zealand, and as the *Maoriland Worker's* natural authority on the subject.[20] It also helped that Josephs spent around £1 a month on advertising with the paper. From March 1911 through to late 1913, Josephs ran weekly adverts that listed a vast supply of pamphlets, books, and newspapers—such as *Freedom*, Goldman's *Mother Earth*, the US-based *Agitator*, and Aldred's *Herald of Revolt* and *The Spur*. Commenting on these adverts, the September 1912 edition of *Freedom* stated: "our comrade, P. Josephs, of Wellington, New Zealand, has succeeded, almost single-handed, in building up an agency for the distribution of Anarchist literature on quite a large scale."[21] Immediately orders and enquiries "began to flow in, the business increasing so quickly that he had not enough stock to keep up with it. This was soon remedied, and larger advertisements brought still bigger business."[22]

Larger advertisements were an understatement. Starting in May 1912 and under the banner 'Headquarters for Anarchist Literature: Library of Anarchism,' double-column directories of anarchist literature swamped smaller adverts for health potions, piano repairs, and hotel holidays. "Attention is called to the big advt. in this issue relating to books handled by the indefatigable P. Joseph [sic]," wrote the *Maoriland Worker*. "Mr. Joseph is in close touch with the American and British publishers of anarchist literature, and sells the same for propaganda and not for profit."[23] Over ninety titles were listed, categorized into sections such as "Works by Peter Kropotkin," "Dramatic Works," "Free Speech

Series," and "Paper and Magazines."[24] Even this was only a small sample of his collection. "All those who are desirous of studying the Anarchist Philosophy in its various phases," wrote Josephs, could send for a four-page list of books and pamphlets on sale, "the variety of which is a striking testimony to the interest he has aroused in Anarchism."[25] A letter to Keel confirmed the claim, stating: "I have sold every pamphlet of the 12 1/2 dozen you sent me... those are certainly very acceptable."[26]

Despite his recent bankruptcy, the sale of literature was not benefiting Josephs financially. "I am not distributing anarchist literature for profit, I am selling all pamphlets for marked price," confided Josephs to Keel, and as the *Maoriland Worker* noted, the "Library of Anarchism, in which some of the finest books printed are offered for sale by Mr. P. Joseph [sic] whose work in this connection is one of pure love for breadth and truth. The prices are bedrock prices."[27] However, his labour garnished rewards of a different kind. Thanks to his spreading of free literature and the *Maoriland Worker's* willingness to give anarchism space on its pages, Josephs continued to pool a steady stream of subscribers to *Freedom*. In 1911 alone he forwarded Keel the names of eight new subscribers in the Wellington region, including W. Hindmarsh (son of prominent labour lawyer Alfred Hindmarsh) and Carl Mumme (a socialist and antimilitarist of German origin who would go on to deliver talks on behalf of the Freedom Group in 1913). A year later he had ten more—a roll call of influential syndicalists that included Robert Semple, John Dowdall, John Dowgray, and Paddy Webb, as well as the Wobblies who had split from the Christchurch NZSP, Stanley Roscoe and C. Shepherd.[28]

It seems Josephs' constant canvassing was bearing fruit. Due to his efforts, international anarchist material was reaching the far corners of the colony. At its peak in 1913, Josephs could count on literature being distributed around the country thanks to agents Harry 'Red' Toovey and Mathew Alach (Auckland), Syd Kingsford (Christchurch), and E.A. Brown (Invercargill). He also had individual subscribers in smaller centres like Blenheim.[29] *Freedom* account books also show that in 1913, W. Harrison of Auckland was ordering over £2 of books and pamphlets. These were not marginalised individuals on the fringes of the labour movement—Toovey was prominent in the Auckland IWW, and Kingsford was an antimilitarist in the Passive Resisters' Union (PRU), a powerful orator, and Literature Secretary of the Christchurch IWW.[30]

However, these transnational influences went both ways. News of the New Zealand labour movement was being studied and shared internationally. Josephs gave *Freedom* constant updates of developments in the New Zealand labour movement, both in his personal letters and by forwarding copies of the *Maoriland Worker* to the collective. Keel and others were kept abreast of arbitration activity through such means. "Things are getting a little lively in NZ," wrote Josephs. "Several unions have already withdrawn from the arbitration Court and several are discussing about their withdrawal too, so it seems that we are confronted with a great change in the labour movement here."[31] He was also sending material to Nettlau—*Freedom* member, avid collector of anarchist ephemera from around the world and author of a multi-volume history of the movement. "This little lot is so far all I can get," wrote Josephs, "but I have been promised a lot more. I will try and send it to you next week."[32] Although exactly what he sent has not been preserved, in all likelihood it would have been radical material relating to the situation in New Zealand—a local pamphlet perhaps, or possibly the *Maoriland Worker*. Nettlau's *Die Geschichte Des Anarchismus* (The History of Anarchism, which includes a page on New Zealand) notes "local worker's papers" and a pamphlet issued by the Wellington Anti-Conscription League "have reached *Freedom* since 1911"—the same year of Josephs' note to Nettlau.[33]

In recognition of his efforts, Josephs' work was promoted abroad by *Freedom* as "an object lesson to those who are sometimes only too ready to sit down and bemoan their own impotence."[34]

The "political crossroads" of New Zealand—a socialist stepping-stone that saw organizers on their way to Australia and San Francisco step off ships and "onto the soap-box"—also left its mark on the wider movement.[35] After his stint in New Zealand and Australia, Tom Mann "completely lost confidence in various Arbitration Acts," and returned to Europe convinced of the bankruptcy of arbitration, state socialism and parliamentary action. "In the colonies supposedly ruled by labour governments, he found pitiful situations for the workers' emancipation, and he returned thoroughly averse to parliamentarism... Only economic organization, with or without social legislation, can achieve things."[36] Articles in *La Vie Ouvriére*, the journal of the French anarcho-syndicalist Confédération Générale du Travail (CGT), and his formation in Britain of the Industrial Syndicalist Educationalist League with

Guy Bowman, illustrate that his New Zealand experience played a part in the development of revolutionary syndicalism abroad.[37]

New Zealand labour relations also confirmed and strengthened the international anarchist critique of state socialism, "a new proof of the truth which we have advocated." *Mother Earth* carried numerous articles on the "Eldorado of reformers and State worshippers," noting in 1911 that New Zealand "toilers are subjected to a straightjacket bound more tightly than is the case in any other country. This despotism with State Socialist tendencies is the faithful lackey of capital in a greater degree than any government of Europe or America."[38] Again, thanks to *Mother Earth*, anarchists abroad could deepen their diatribes by drawing on the bitter example of the 1912 Waihi Strike. "The strike arbitration laws of New Zealand—so enthusiastically hailed by American reformers as an effective solution of labor troubles—is beginning to show results that fill its champions with anxiety and fear," began an article documenting the violent outcome of the miners' battle with arbitration, the employers, and the state:

> For a whole week the myrmidons [warriors] of capital and government carried on the orgy of violence, and during that time 1,800 men and women were driven forcibly from the place, till Waihi now resembles a deserted village. The masters, aided by the authorities, have finally succeeded in establishing the peace of Warsaw in Waihi.[39]

The January 1913 edition of *Freedom* also carried an article on 'Waihi's Black Week,' and it is likely similar New Zealand news was exchanged amongst English and foreign speaking papers. "Leaflets, pamphlets and journals were par excellence the means of communication between anarchist groups," writes Hermia Oliver. "The circulation [of anarchist news] was thus geographically very wide."[40]

In Scotland too, Aldred's *The Spur* reported on the New Zealand situation, describing the country's prevailing militarism and gifting the New Zealand state a sordid claim to fame. "Of all British Dominions, for scientifically suppressing revolutionary thought the New Zealand Government is the worst," wrote *The Spur*.[41] For these international newspapers, labour regulation and state sanctions in the form of New Zealand's arbitration law was no model to be mimicked.

Another example of a New Zealand influence abroad (and a further transnational link to *Freedom*) is the visit to London by New Zealand

Wobbly, Percy Short. After the Great Strike of 1913, Short left the country to "get an insight into the European movement."[42] But while abroad he also imparted knowledge of his own. As well as replying in person to a letter received by the Auckland IWW from a syndicalist publication in Europe, Short was interviewed by Nettlau, who was interested in hearing news of the Great Strike and arbitration firsthand. Having been on the committee of the *Industrial Unionist* and having penned a number of articles in the Maori language for its pages (extremely unique at the time), Short was a well-qualified interviewee.

Although in his interview Short touched on antimilitarism (including a hunger strike of PRU militants in Lyttelton) and the Maori response to syndicalist propaganda, it was the trade union movement and the behaviour of the conservative organizations that interested [Nettlau] the most:

Q. And how are the strikes in your 'workers' paradise', the 'country without strikes and lock-outs', as our social reformers in Europe like to call it?

A. The strikes are growing, both in terms of numbers and in intensity [the interview was conducted a few weeks after the end of the Great Strike].

Q. And the law on strikes, which makes them illegal?

A. The compulsory Arbitration Act has had its head smashed in New Zealand.[43]

"We would have liked to continue our conversation," wrote Nettlau, but "comrade Short's visit wasn't only about passing on information, but also to obtain information."[44] It appears Short then resumed his syndicalist tour of duty, only to arrive home to a New Zealand steeped in militarism.

Lola Ridge—anarchist and poet with "an intense personality and revolutionary zeal"—is another interesting example of antipodean outreach.[45] After emigrating from Ireland at the age of five, Ridge spent her formative years in New Zealand, growing up in the West Coast mining town of Hokitika. Despite motherhood and an unhappy marriage, Ridge still found time to write poetry, and after leaving New Zealand in 1903, her work was widely celebrated in the United States. Befriending Goldman, she became active in the New York anarchist movement and was an early advocate of women's rights, gay rights, and the rights of people of colour, Jews, and other immigrant groups.[46]

As well as her day-to-day activism, Ridge kept up her political prose as a vehicle for social change, aimed at capturing the hearts and minds of both workers and those of the literary milieu. Her authentic experience of working class life in New Zealand was put to good use. Ridge's poem *The Martyrs of Hell* graced a 1909 cover of *Mother Earth*, while another work, *Frank Little at Calvary*, publicized the violent death of IWW organizer Frank Little (who, in 1917, was tortured, castrated, and lynched from the side of a Butte, Montana bridge for organizing workers of the Anaconda Copper Company). Her cultural activism also helped rally funds in defence of imprisoned anarchists like Nicola Sacco and Bartolomeo Vanzetti—a case regarded by many as the largest miscarriage of justice in the US and which saw an intense transnational campaign for their release, including the formation of a Sacco-Vanzetti Defence Committee in Auckland.[47] Ridge's *Stone Face*, a poster-poem about jailed unionist Tom Mooney that sold in the hundreds of thousands and swamped the streets of America, "is perhaps the most widely distributed poem by any New Zealander."[48] Her published collections of poetry won the most prized literary awards in the US, yet sadly, her work remains relatively unknown in New Zealand.

Ridge's link to New Zealand, like that of the many itinerant workers and organizers who passed through the country, points to a transnationalism that goes beyond the predominant understanding of international influence—one that has typically been viewed by New Zealand historians as mainly being inbound. Those who brought ideas into New Zealand also left with them modified or clarified. As a result, New Zealand's labour relations and the activities of local anarchists such as Josephs fits into a wider, global context—one that saw a period of intense labour strife in Europe and the United States before 1914, and the birth of anarchist labour organizations like the CGT in France, Spain's Confederación Nacional del Trabajo (CNT), and the Federación Obrera Regional Argentina in Argentina. The development of anarchism in New Zealand after 1904 (like the anarchist and syndicalist movement in general) was transnational, and deepened simultaneously with the international upsurge of workers' militancy and the anarchist movement abroad.

CHAPTER 7

NO WAR BUT CLASS WAR

Besides the critique of state socialism, arbitration, and trade unionism, another affinity that New Zealand anarchists shared with their comrades abroad was antimilitarism. Resistance to compulsory military training and conscription was a major issue for the radical Left in New Zealand, and much energy was spent on challenging it—before, during, and after the strikes of 1912 and 1913. Alongside his distribution of anarchist literature, Josephs was also a prominent antimilitarist, filling the role of secretary of the Wellington Anti-Militarist League. His antimilitarism, his constant anarchist agitation, and the radicalizing, fast-paced years immediately preceding the First World War would culminate with the founding of the Freedom Group and the Great Strike of 1913.

New Zealand antimilitarism was born out of opposition to the Defence Act of 1909, an Act that "represented New Zealand's attempt to re-organize its defence forces along the lines agreed to at the Imperial Naval and Military Conference held in London in July and August of that year."[1] It made registration and military training compulsory for males between fourteen and thirty years of age, and enabled magistrates to deal out a considerable amount of punishment to those who did not.

As well as more temperate church groups who aimed "to appeal to the middle class by focusing on issues around the militarization of youth and society in general," socialists of most shades rejected compulsory military training. But in contrast to their unlikely comrades, they rejected militarism for decidedly anti-capitalist reasons.[2] The FOL viewed compulsory military training as "a weapon of capitalist imperialism" which could be used against the interests of workers and the working class itself, both "domestically and internationally."[3] Instead, FOL and NZSP organizers took antimilitarist agitation to the only class they believed could end capitalist militarism—the working class.

Alongside his erstwhile comrades of the NZSP, Josephs dived head-first into the struggle. For Josephs, compulsory military training and conscription was both a capitalist weapon and a form of state oppression. As well as stocking his shelves with antimilitarist material, he used the pages of the *Maoriland Worker* to put forward a decidedly anarchist position on militarism in its New Zealand form. In a double-column article called "The General Strike As a Weapon Against Conscription," Josephs analysed the arguments for and against military training. "The land-owners, big farmers, manufacturers, and large storekeepers own 95% of the nation's wealth," he said, "it is therefore to their interest to have a well trained army to protect their interests."[4] As a way of fighting conscription and "that section who monopolised the nation's wealth, and thereby denied the masses of their original rights to the wealth they created," Josephs urged miners and the FOL to call a general strike. "Many will say such actions would be too harsh," he added. "What have the Government done by passing such an Act? The Government have ignored you. They forced conscription on you suddenly, and if they have the right to commit such a harsh act, it is also right for the workers to do exactly as their opponents have done to them."[5]

He also lambasted the NZSP, arguing that their legalistic demands of an immediate repeal of the Act, because it was passed without consultation, was contradictory:

I must say frankly it does not matter whether there are laws in favour of it or not—laws were always made for the protection of one class against another, even if the laws were made by a Labour Party or Socialist Party... The Socialist Party, being against such laws that are made in favour of one class to oppress another, cannot conscientiously use legal means in opposing such laws; it would be like stretching a piece of elastic that goes back with tremendous reactionary force. We must once and for all realise that the workers must find means independent of those in accordance with the existing laws, knowing the laws always have worked against them.[6]

True to his internationalism, Josephs made it clear that "the deprivation of the workers' wealth and rights exist in every country alike. Our enemies are not abroad. They exist in our midst."[7]

The apex of antimilitarism in New Zealand was Christchurch, where groups such as the Anti-Militarist League (formed in 1910 by Louise Christie), the National Peace Council (NPC) of Charles Mackie, and the militant Passive Resisters' Union (PRU) conducted antimilitarist agitation in the form of pamphlets, mass meetings, and direct action. These umbrella organizations spread nationwide, and when the Wellington branch of the Anti-Militarist League was revived in April 1912, Josephs was elected secretary. In this role, Josephs advertised and conducted their monthly meetings, networked with the NPC and the PRU, and organized guest speakers, including one public meeting at Wellington's Post Office Square that featured soapboxing from Hickey, Ross, McCullough, and Eagle.[8]

Despite starting well, Josephs lamented in a July letter to Mackie, "the League in Wellington is making slow progress."[9] However, after the government began to increase its imprisonment of those who failed to register under the Act, and a national conference of antimilitarists in Wellington during November solidified resistance, Josephs—somewhat more buoyantly—wrote in December, "there are signs of a good movement in Wellington. Mr. P. O'Regan and Mr. Bedford who have been very prominent some time ago have again come to light and the future is very promising."[10]

The mix of religious, liberal, and militant working-class organizations meant antimilitarist activism appeared in different forms. For Mackie and the NPC, the sole task was one of public education. But for labour militants like Josephs and the PRU—who, although they were antimilitarists, were not necessarily pacifists—such methods seemed painstakingly slow and were easily ignored by the government.[11] The militant resistance of the PRU and Josephs' advocacy of the general strike sometimes clashed with the conciliatory stance of their Christian cohorts. This tension is reflected in Josephs' last letter to Mackie, which stated rather bluntly: "your suggestion is an excellent one although I disagree with some of your methods to get the act repealed, still I would assist, even if it only serves as a lesson to prove its fallacy."[12] And in the *Maoriland Worker*: "the meetings held to protest against the Act are a little too respectable. Nothing will be gained by such methods. You want to show your direct power against the governing classes, in order to make them realise the danger in passing such laws in the future."[13]

Yet despite disagreements over methods, anarchists like Josephs remained active in the broad campaign. As a PRU delegate and "a fairly intelligent sort of slave," Kingsford penned a stinging letter in the *Evening Post* that openly denounced militarism in the language of class war, and gives us a sense of his soapbox socialism:

> Not content with robbing my class of the major portion of its product, the robber class has the colossal impudence to demand that the sons of the robbed workers shall don a uniform, shoulder a rifle, and be prepared to defend the possessions of the robbers... What does it matter to me if the robbers sometimes fall out and quarrel over the division of the spoil wrung from the workers? The point is that I am robbed with impartiality by the capitalist class, no matter what country I am in, or what nation I happen to belong to. To me, no country is so superior to another that I want to get shot in its defence. I prefer to work for the time when national barriers will be thrown down, and the workers united for the purpose of evading a system of society which causes war. General Sherman said "War is Hell." Let the war-makers go to war, and fight their own battles.[14]

In similar terms, Jones argued, "war is the result of the present capitalist system. I affirm that incentives of profit and loss are the real factors... we are told we are fighting German militarism. Do we believe our newspapers?"[15]

The relationships forged between anarchists and others in the struggle against militarism were obviously long lasting. On an IWW organizing tour of New Zealand in 1913, Barker held numerous joint meetings with Josephs in Wellington and also with the PRU in Christchurch (including a street meeting that saw both him and Kingsford fined for obstruction).[16] During the same tour, the Christchurch IWW was revived as Local 2, with Kingsford as Press Correspondent and Ernie Kear, late secretary of the PRU, elected as Secretary. These relationships and their resulting activities were having some effect. Anarchists like Kingsford, alongside the highly successful PRU and other antimilitarist groups, inspired many youths to refuse training and to challenge the legality of law itself—prompting Minister of Defence James Allen to exclaim that the rule of law was blatantly violated by "regular young anarchists" out to "break down the [Defence] Act altogether." He was increasingly dismayed that antimilitarists were prepared to "adopt any means to obtain their ends."[17]

Yet despite success in the south, by mid-1913 the Wellington Anti-Militarist League seems to have been on the decline. "I must say things in Wellington is [sic] very quiet it is impossible to get a proper meeting together," bemoaned Josephs, who also lamented the fact that other Wellington antimilitarists were calling meetings without notifying the League—fragmenting the fight. "If we are going on like this," he concluded, "we'll achieve nothing. I'll try and get a meeting together shortly to test the feelings of those who are concerned... but I am almost certain of its failure... we'll see."[18]

Josephs need not have worried, for the wave of syndicalist agitation that had been gathering speed since 1908 was about to subsume anti-militarism in open class warfare. And this time around, Josephs could organize on his own terms.

"A matter that should have an effect in clearing the somewhat misty atmosphere in this city is the movement to form an Anarchist Group in Wellington," wrote the *Maoriland Worker*, "for it will provide those who accept the Anarchist philosophy with the place where they belong... we understand that this will be the first Anarchist group formed in the history of New Zealand."[19] One week later, the paper carried the historic news:

At No. 4 Willis Street on July 9 [1913], a meeting was held to form an Anarchist Group, to be called the Freedom Group. Its object is the self-education of its members and the propagation of Anarchist Principles. It was decided to have weekly meetings, commencing at 8pm every Wednesday, at Josephs & Co's rooms, 4 Willis St. The subject for discussion next week is 'What methods should we adopt to change the present system?'... those interested will always find a warm welcome, and visitors are invited to take part in the discussions.[20]

Unfortunately, we have little material on the group, its members, or for how long the collective existed. The little evidence that does exist however, suggests that Josephs played a key role, and that the group was popular. Their weekly anarchist discussion nights had "a good attendance of comrades," featured "lively discussion" and many questions—covering topics such as "Marxian Fallacies," "Parliament and its Relations to the Labour Movement," and "Defects of Industrial Organization."[21]

Two lectures—"How to Solve the Labour Problem in New Zealand" and "Will Social Democracy Succeed in the Economic Emancipation of the People?"—were given by Wellington cabinet maker and unionist, Carl Hinrich Andreas Mumme (known as Charles).[22] He was certainly qualified to speak on such topics, having been secretary of the Furniture Workers' Union in 1897 and a founding member of the NZSP (at one stage he was on the executive committee of the Wellington branch). He was a staunch antimilitarist involved in various Wellington campaigns, and also represented the Amalgamated Society of Carpenters and Joiners (ASCJ) on the Wellington branch of the FOL in 1911.[23] These were positions of some influence, and although speculative, it is interesting to ponder what kind of reach Mumme and his lectures may have had.

Interestingly, from 1911 onwards Mumme was one of Josephs' *Freedom* subscribers and a likely convert to anarchism as a result. As well as his lectures, two other examples back such a claim. Not only did he lead a breakaway of carpenters and joiners "opposed to compulsory unionism and its tyranny" out of the ASCJ (which, in February 1913, formed the rival New Zealand Brotherhood of Carpenters and Joiners, with Mumme as secretary), he also did some anarchist recruiting of his own. A month before the first meeting of the Freedom Group, Mumme had signed up six new subscribers to *Freedom*.[24] It seems his role in the Group was more than that of a guest speaker.

On a winter's night in August, the Freedom Group and friends stoked the embers of revolutionary thought by pondering questions accumulated over the previous month, illustrating a breadth of topics and the development of stimulating anarchist pedagogy:

> a very lively discussion took place on a number of questions, viz. "Has political action been beneficial to the working class?" "Shall we have to pass through a socialist state to reach anarchy?" "Is religion a barrier to progress?" "Does woman recognize her independence?" "Do the anarchists accept the principles of the economic interpretation of history?" and others.[25]

These forums of anarchist philosophy must have been popular, for the meetings soon shifted from Josephs' tailor shop to the considerably larger Socialist Hall on Manners Street.

The Freedom Group also followed another NZSP tradition, the social, although with a twist. In September, Josephs made arrangements with Comrades Garlick, Reynolds, and Bailey of the NZSP to hire the Socialist Hall for an event of a kind never before experienced in New Zealand.[26] Billed as an evening in the "form of an Anarchist-Communist society, where one is equal to another, where no criminals, no officials, and no authority exists," attendees could enjoy short speeches, readings of prominent authors, recitations and musical entertainment, "enjoying for at least one evening the benefits of a perfectly free society."[27] Tickets were available from Josephs, other members of the Freedom Group, or from the Socialist Hall.

The event itself was held in "real anarchist style." Upon entering the Hall, revellers found that decorated tables "formed a circle, and the absence of a chairman did away with the formality usually found in Socialist and other meetings." Between dancing and ditties, the anarchist position was explained and future talks planned, "everyone expressing the hope that a similar function would be held in the near future." The *Maoriland Worker's* report finished with the Freedom Group "especially thank[ing] the ladies and other comrades whose aid made the meeting such a huge success."[28]

It is near impossible to measure the impact of the Freedom Group and its events on the workers of Wellington. However, the fact that around 120 people attended the "anarchist communist" evening gives some sense of the popularity of the collective in the Wellington milieu.[29] Likewise, when Tom Barker swept through the country on his organizing tour in August/September, he relied on Josephs and the Freedom Group for aid: "With the help of our anarchist friend and comrade P. Josephs" wrote Barker from Wellington, "I had 11 propaganda meetings in 14 days."[30] At the very least, the collective was obviously a visible and vibrant feature of Wellington's working-class counter-culture, and facilitated thought-provoking (even politically transformative) conversation. For it should be noted that anarchist groups were not simple replicas of socialist parties, but intentionally transformative spaces, based on a shared affinity and the desire to live and act in the most libertarian ways possible—a place to put anarchist ideas into practice. To be a member of such a group would have meant more than receiving a party card. As a result, the emergence of the Freedom Group in 1913 signified a real advance in New Zealand anarchist praxis. This advance, and its radicalizing influence, was the result of Josephs 'indefatigable' efforts.

The revelry would be short-lived however, for a few weeks later one of New Zealand's most bitter and far reaching industrial disputes, the Great Strike of 1913, broke out on the wharves of Wellington. When the Union Steam Ship Company aggressively refused to pay travelling time for shipwrights (a number of whom had earlier de-registered from the ICA), watersiders downed tools in protest. At the same time in Huntly, 560 miners struck after 16 fellow-workers (including members of the union executive) were dismissed by the Taupiri Coal Company.[31] Strike action soon spread; without waiting for official sanction, miners on the West Coast took wildcat strike action and helped shut down the ports of Westport and Greymouth. Auckland ports, as well as most of the city, came to a complete stop thanks to sympathy strikes, resulting in a general strike in the north. "Such was the mood of militancy" writes Moriarty-Patten, "that inmates of an old persons' home struck in protest about the quality of food, and inmates at Lyttelton Gaol formed a union and tried to affiliate to the United Federation of Labour."[32]

Rather than one unified action, the Great Strike was cluster of strikes predominately initiated by the rank-and-file, involving some 16,000 workers, monster demonstrations, and running battles with 'Massey's Cossacks'—volunteer special constables mainly recruited from farm workers, dubbed in honour of then-Prime Minister and leader of the Reform Party, William Massey. Neither were they restricted to simple economic disputes of pay. Like the class war at Waihi, the Great Strike was a dynamic and often violent power play between capital and labour, one that dramatically changed the demeanour of social relations in the colony. Arbitration was out, and for an exciting and empowering period, direct action was the means of choice for the rank-and-file worker.

Challenges to authority came thick and fast. When the strikers were refused a permit to use Wellington's Basin Reserve for a mass meeting, the crowd of over 1,000 simply smashed down the gates, stormed the Basin, and held it anyway—the police could do nothing but sit helplessly by and watch. Again, when mounted specials tried to clear a crowd on Buckle Street, "two women, stubbornly and with loud protests, refused to budge from the positions they had taken up on the footpath"—defying law and order and thrilling the crowd in the process.[33] "Prosecutions for offences against the authority of the State were a prominent feature of the cases arising from the strike," notes Donald Anderson—nervous labour leaders became "extremely concerned" over the lack of control over "obstreperous wharfies, whose confidence was unbounded."[34]

As tensions between strikers and specials hardened, conflicts began to escalate. Gunsmiths and ironmongers sold out of pistols as the demeanour of the strike soured. The mere existence of a strikebreaking body, let alone the aggressive and unpopular show of force on the part of the specials, "allowed considerable opportunity for violence and abuse."[35] Clashes between the two sides finally climaxed on 3 November, when a large crowd of Wellington strikers and "anti-authority elements from the neighbouring Te Aro slums" had fire hoses turned on them after refusing to disperse. In turn, they overturned pavers, gathered bottles and pales, and besieged a barrack of mounted specials with their new-found loot. On the orders of Police Commissioner John Cullen (recently returned from perfecting provocative tactics in Waihi), the specials responded with a baton-wielding cavalry charge. "If they won't go," yelled Cullen, "ride over the top of them."[36] And that is what they did:

the mounted specials... charge[d] the crowd, which included many women, children and elderly people, allegedly after shots were fired at the police. People were batoned and trampled to the ground, and some of the specials almost certainly fired weapons. Cullen denied this, and secured censorship of the *Dominion's* account of the incident; but it is certain that shots were fired at the specials from windows and under verandahs.[37]

The crowd, taking refuge under "verandahs, in doorways, in recesses which men on horseback could not reach," fought back. "The shower of missiles, including the odd bullet, continued."[38] "Through the darkness fire-arms flashed and thundered," wrote the *Dominion's* Pat Lawlor, whose editor—alongside Cullen—tried to convince him that the gunfire had not come from the specials. Despite submitting his eyewitness account and sticking to his "guns about the guns," Lawlor "was heartbroken though to find, next day that the story was all in favour of the police. The Editor... had passed by the evidence of his excited junior as against the declarations of the Commissioner of Police."[39]

Despite altered press accounts and the presence of police, the strikers stayed solid. Actions accelerated. Two days later, both sides clashed again. The Battle of Featherston Street saw strikers and their sympathizers attack a column of 800 specials escorting racehorses to the Wellington wharves. Bricks, iron bolts, road metal, and anything loose were hurled at the mounted specials—one tram-driver even rammed his tram into the rear of the column—only to be met with equally vicious hooves and baton blows.[40] These riotous power struggles led one member of parliament to describe the street fighting as "a system of Mexican revolt and civil war," while the NZ Truth claimed the strike "would lead a stranger to imagine that he had been transported to a country at war, or at the least to a place which was in a state of anarchy."[41]

Wobblies were especially active during the strike, producing weekly editions of the Unionist and speaking from soapboxes around the country. One speech by Barker—described in court as "one of the most dangerous made in the course of the industrial trouble, and probably one of the most dangerous ever uttered in the Dominion"—saw him jailed for sedition.[42] Barker and other Wobblies, like Leo Woods in Thames, were prominent members of strike committees, while the IWW, on a whole, endeavoured to make life hell for specials. Wobblies wielded more than words—covering roads with barbed wire, marbles, and trip ropes, and rolling rocks down the banks of Ngauranga Gorge as specials travelled towards Wellington. Once the specials had arrived, Wobblies joined a throng of strikers that attacked their headquarters. "With a Maori war cry," writes Derby, the strikers "stampeded the horses and tossed the barricade materials into the harbour."[43]

Anarchists were also in the thick of things. Prebble wrote that rumours of the Freedom Group having "street fights with coppers" perhaps relates to the events in November, and Len Richardson mentions that acts of sabotage on the West Coast were the work of an active "anarchist fringe of the IWW" (although it should be noted that related police reports make no mention of anarchists, only the IWW—the label of anarchist is Richardson's).[44] Another police report shows that Josephs was definitely involved in the action. "Being an out and out socialist," wrote Detective-Sergeant McIlveney, "he took part in connection with the last waterside workers' strike, and occasionally expressed his views publicly from a platform in the vicinity of the Queen's wharf."[45] On December 14, Mumme also spoke publicly at Newtown Park, addressing an enthusiastic crowd of around 2,000 who had braved the boisterous weather for news of the strike's progress.[46] As well as soapboxing, it is likely that Josephs, Mumme, and others in the Freedom Group would have been amongst the swarms of strikers distributing pamphlets, further adding an anarchist voice to the discontent.

Josephs also used the columns of the capitalist press to express his sympathy. A letter to the *Evening Post*, criticizing the formation of a Defence Committee to protect the women and children of Khandallah (his new suburb of residence), questioned the unnecessary scare mongering:

> I strongly protest such action. I believe it to be a shame and a disgrace to raise a scare amongst the people here without any cause whatsoever. Those who never dreamt of being in any way molested by anyone while the industrial crisis is on will now suspect any harmless object they may meet… My children, who always walked freely through Khandallah any time of the day or evening, are now frightened to move out of the house in case they meet those special guards, who are supposed to protect them.[47]

The employers certainly had protection—in the form of the New Zealand state. Before long naval ships berthed in Auckland had their guns trained on the city, machine guns were strategically placed in pockets of Wellington, and soldiers with naked bayonets protected both specials and 'free' labour to re-open the docks. By December strike leaders were arrested for sedition, localized strikes collapsed as workers drifted back to work, and the coalition of government and employers gained the upper hand. The veneer of democracy was resumed under the cover of military might. The Freedom Group, which began with such promise, completely disappears from the record after the Great Strike. Who knows what the Group could have achieved had it been given more time to develop.

CHAPTER 8

PARASITES, ANARCHISTS, AND OTHER IWW TYPES

The intentions of the New Zealand state during the Great Strike of 1913, why the strike was unsuccessful, and its effect on the New Zealand labour movement, have been the topic of much discussion. Bert Roth and Richard Hill argue that employers helped escalate the strike in order to crush the syndicalist upsurge and its more militant elements: "their reaction to the stop work meeting in Wellington, when many others had been held before without repercussion, suggests that they manipulated the trade unions into a fight they were unlikely to win, and were supported by a Government who was determined to use all means necessary to support the employers."[1] However Fairburn believes that this was not the case, that there is not enough evidence to draw such a conclusion, and on the contrary, employers had been incredibly tolerant of previous wildcat strikes.

Yet the Employers' Federation had clearly been preparing for some kind of showdown, publishing a pamphlet in 1912 titled "Organizing and Defence Fund Schemes," and establishing, in early 1913, "a huge fund to fight the organized workers... to combat Socialism, Syndicalism, and Anarchy." In August, the bosses' Federation also organized secret meetings to gather a possible reserve of strikebreakers.[2] The state's infiltration of unions and the passing of a host of anti-labour laws before the Strike (including harsher penalties for striking and the outlawing of aggressive picketing) also suggests "that the employers and the government were lining up for a fight with the militants."[3]

While the New Zealand government's intention to smash the labour movement during the Great Strike is questioned by some, there is no disputing the state's war on revolutionary syndicalism after New

Zealand entered the First World War. For despite its liberal facade, New Zealand was one of the most stringent suppressors of dissent in the western world. To denounce government at that time spelled disaster— it was dangerous enough to be a Christian pacifist, let alone a member of an explicitly anarchist collective. As moments of crisis made clear, New Zealand's democracy was simply an iron hand in a velvet glove.

Regardless of whether the Freedom Group folded because of the Great Strike, or due to state suppression during the Great War, it must have come as a blow for Josephs. After years of toil he had managed to bring together an organized group of anarchists in New Zealand—not an easy feat considering the social and moral norms as governed by the mainstream media. However, after the Strike and despite timorous times, Josephs kept up his transnational anarchist agitation (albeit in more clandestine forms). As a committee member of the Khandallah Literary and Debating Society, he may have propagated anarchism in an academic setting that—although a far cry from the "political university" that was the Wellington wharves—was at the very least, less hazardous.[4] Well into 1915, willing workers could still purchase anarchist literature from Josephs, although the heightened atmosphere of jingoism and surveillance during the First World War made it extremely dangerous to do so. In fact, it was this state of affairs—and the watchful gaze of a censor—that would lead to Josephs' targeting and put an end to his anarchist activity in New Zealand.

Around the globe, the First World War "devoured, channelled, and co-opted the discontent unleashed by the storm of industrial and class conflict."[5] This diffusion was helped along locally by a state at the forefront of using wartime regulations for political ends. For the national coalition government headed by Massey, socialist activity represented the threat of larger resistance to its involvement in the First World War, or even worse, a possible repeat of the growth experienced by militant labour leading up to the revolutionary moments of 1913.[6] The government took measures to clamp down on any non-conformist activity it deemed seditious, using the pretence of war conditions to further cement its hold. The resulting War Regulations Act empowered the executive branch of the government to regulate all aspects of national life without reference to Parliament.[7] What initially began as regulations of a purely military nature was soon extended to cover dissent of the political kind.

Rather tellingly, those convicted of publishing information deemed valuable to the enemy were fined amounts ranging from 5/- to £10, while anyone who publicly criticized the actions of the New Zealand government was fined £100 or received twelve months' imprisonment with hard labour. Even the British government, who New Zealand still turned to for guidance, "was more tolerant of criticism than the Massey administration and did not readily initiate prosecutions for sedition."[8] However, in New Zealand, seditious activity was a category of elastic dimensions, defined by the state in such a way as to encompass a broad range of activity—including anything deemed critical of the New Zealand government, the war effort, and conscription. Strikes in essential war industries were outlawed and defined as seditious. Socialist objections to conscription, Christians who argued that militarism was contrary to their religious beliefs, and sometimes harmless banter between friends, were all defined as seditious. By the war's end, 287 people had been charged with sedition or disloyalty: 208 were convicted and 71 sent to prison.[9] The New Zealand government was living up to *The Spur's* claim as the greatest suppressor of revolutionary thought.

Police or detectives could be relied upon to attend every public labour or anti-conscription meeting, which made anti-war and socialist agitation—publicly or privately—extremely difficult. Anarchists and the IWW were particularly targeted, due to their advocacy of direct action at the point of production, the fostering of an oppositional working-class counter-culture, and their radical critique of capitalism. New Zealand's Crown Prosecutor "repeatedly stressed the distinction between sincere objectors… and 'parasites,' 'anarchists,' and other IWW types," and as a result, a number of anarchists and Wobblies were arrested and given maximum jail time under the War Regulations.[10]

Despite being naturalized in 1896 and having spent close to twenty years in the country, police repeatedly raided Carl Mumme's house due to his anarchist/antimilitarist views. In May 1916, detectives found that Mumme's son Harry, then eighteen years old, had not taken part in military training because "as an out and out socialist" Mumme would "never allow his son to serve as a territorial; and that he is prepared to defend the lad against such service at the cost of his life."[11] A week, later the forty-eight-year-old was arrested at work and shipped out to Somes Island, a detention camp situated inside Wellington Harbour. Mumme's wife Margaret and their five children (the youngest being two years old) were not told of his arrest—it took two days for them to find out what had happened.[12] Questioning his internment in a letter to Defence Minister Allen, Mumme declared,

> My principle is this: That I am eager to produce for the welfare of all, that I stand for the greatest happiness for all, that I do not believe in the Mosaic Law nor do I believe in returning evil for evil. If sacrificing my life for Liberty, or for that of anyone else, is a crime, then I can only plead guilty, I will bear my punishment.[13]

Allen replied that his hands were tied. So were Mumme's. It took over three years for him to be released.

The prisoners on Somes Island faced a macabre mix of freedom, boredom, and brutal beatings, thanks to the obstinate commandant Major Dugald Matheson and his guards. Prisoners were often made to exercise until they fainted, put in solitary confinement for meaningless infringements, or taken down to the water's edge and beaten while Matheson watched on. Typical was Matheson's treatment of the "contemptible" Walter Moormeister, a "strike agitator from Waihi," who alleged he was thrown down a stairwell by Matheson, causing a hernia that was not operated on for seventeen days.[14]

Mumme's antimilitarism and his anarchist beliefs ("I do not believe in the principle of electing a [squad] leader always consciously believing that common sense and reason will guide me") ensured a stormy relationship with Matheson's schoolyard militarism. After refusing to address the commandant as 'Sir' and for alluding to mistreatment in letters to his wife—which included the 'hostile' line, "excuse my short note because I cannot write lies and I dare not write the truth"—Mumme was repeatedly punished for insubordination, including forced exercise, bread and water rations for twenty-one days and violent abuse from guards.[15] Matheson—expressing his "utter contempt for a man who is an open enemy of all Governments"— wrote in one report that, although no evidence of conduct hostile to the Camp could be proved, Mumme was "an infidel, a social democratic agitator and an active antimilitarist... posing as a martyr."[16] "On more than one occasion," announced another report, "letters sent out by him were destroyed by the censor on account of references hostile to the authorities responsible for his arrest."[17] In turn, Mumme alleged that he was targeted by guards, and accused "the Commandant of saying that he would do his best to punish him whilst in the Camp for writing to the American Consul [about the treatment of prisoners]."[18]

Mumme was "quite outspoken on Somes Island" confirms his family, "often speaking up for the younger men."[19] Indeed, a number of people—both friend and foe—spoke positively of Mumme's generosity towards others before the Alien Enemy Commission in June 1916. "Mumme is well and favourably known to a very large circle of friends in the city, as an average industrious worker," wrote fellow carpenter and unionist John Brown, while Solomon Gordon added: "I know he has never had any sympathy with Prussian militarism. He was against militarism altogether." The Board concluded that, "although fanatically opposed to militarism," Mumme's "sincerity cannot be doubted," and recommended his release.[20] Yet despite sureties and desperate letters from his near-destitute wife, Mumme remained in detention—his freedom blocked by police and military command. "Mumme is a Socialist apparently of the revolutionary type, and the fact that he stopped his son from attending Territorial parades shows just what he is. Mumme is exactly the type of man who should be deported," wrote one chief detective.[21] While never deported, Mumme was not released from internment until 13 October 1919.[22]

Meanwhile back in Wellington, Wobblies were being herded into landlocked cells. 'Rabid Orator' Joseph Herbert Jones was imprisoned for a speech made to 500 people in Dixon Street. "I want the working class to say to the masters," said Jones, "we don't want war. We won't go to the war." When prominent 1913 striker Charles J. Johnson was arrested in 1917 for having "an enormous amount of IWW literature" in his possession, he was sentenced to twelve months' imprisonment with hard labour.[23] Another militant to receive a twelve-month sentence was Sidney Fournier. Fournier had caused "hostility and ill-will between different classes of His Majesty's subjects" by opposing the Conscription Act and calling on workers to fight the only war that mattered—class war:

> The view of us workers is that we should be fighting the only war in which we can at least become victorious—that is, the class war, or the war between the classes of people who own and control the wealth in all the countries that are now at war, and the people who labour and are exploited by the wealthy classes in all countries. The

truth is this war is being forced on us by conscription, because as we know they take any opportunity that will produce them more wealth and give them more opportunity of oppression, until a peace could be brought about to their advantage, as they conceive it.[24]

When Fournier was arrested he was found to have in his possession a membership card of the IWW, a book on sabotage, a manifesto against conscription, and other "anarchist literature."[25] This, and his speech, was enough to seal his fate. Upon his release, he was blacklisted and prevented from working on the Wellington wharves.

As well as public utterances, private correspondence soon became a target of the state. "Immediately on the outbreak of hostilities a strict telegraph censorship was instituted," wrote Postmaster Joseph Ward, and "a censorship of foreign postal correspondence was also established."[26] Domestic correspondence—both inwards and outwards—was closely monitored, so much so that some gave up on receiving mail entirely. On discovering that almost all of his mail (including Christmas cards) was being withheld, Mackie advised his friends not to bother writing.[27]

So when Josephs penned a letter and mail order to Emma Goldman in September 1915, the machinery of the state was set in motion, sparking "prompt and careful" police surveillance of Josephs himself, the detention of all his mail, and a raid on his home and shop:

> I have to report that [Josephs] is carrying on a tailoring business in 95 Cuba Street, and resides with his wife and family at Khandallah. He is a Russian Jew and has been in business here for several years... As the correspondence clearly shows that Josephs is in receipt of anarchist literature, I would respectfully suggest that the military authorities be asked to furnish us with authority... to search his shop and dwelling.[28]

On Friday October 8, Josephs felt the force of the state firsthand. He was arrested and "detained all day in the 'cooler' until 4 o'clock in the afternoon when he was released without any charge being placed against him."[29] While he stewed in a Wellington jail cell, two detectives "searched Josephs' shop in Cuba Street and took possession of all books and papers, on anarchism and socialism, found on the premises." They then repeated their search at his Khandallah home. Letters, account books, forty magazines and books in foreign print, eleven newspapers in foreign print (including Chinese anarchist circulars that perhaps were for distribution in Wellington's Chinatown), and over fifty books and pamphlets in English were confiscated, "most of which appear to be against government of any kind; and, are advocating for what is termed a 'General Strike' as the best means of obtaining individual liberty."[30] Police also found a swag of prepared speeches on anarchism and socialism written inside the pages of Josephs' contributions book, confirming that he was a regular propagator of anarchism in the public realm.

The police report and confiscated material held at Archives New Zealand appears as new as the day it was filed, and makes for fascinating reading. Detective-Sergeant James McIlveney (who also arrested Mumme) was very thorough, and made an extensive list of the titles in Josephs' possession. His collection of revolutionary reading included a number of books by Kropotkin, Reclus, Morris, Bernard Shaw, and Daniel De Leon (among others); Aldred's Bakunin Press pamphlet series; works on free speech; and New Zealand newspapers such as the *Industrial Unionist* and the PRU's *Repeal*.[31] The neatly handwritten letter from Josephs to Goldman included an account payment (complete with a preserved Te Aro Post Office money order form); invoices from the Mother Earth Publishing Association that mentions B. Raskin as a New Zealand subscriber of *Mother Earth*; and a personal order for two new books advertised in Goldman's paper.

As well as holding a considerable stash of anarchist literature, it appears Josephs' shop was, or had been, the Wellington headquarters of the IWW. Police found "a number of unused official membership books, rubber stamps, and other gear used in connection with that constitution," as well as IWW pamphlets and papers. According to *Direct Action* (the paper of the Australian IWW), any postage to the Wellington local was received care of Josephs, meaning he was an active supporter of the New Zealand IWW, if not a member.[32] Indeed, in an earlier letter to Keel, Josephs mentioned that a number of individuals interested in anarchism tended to devote their energies to "IWW work"—work he believed "is certainly also necessary."[33] Such a scenario illustrates the often-blurred lines between anarchist and Wobbly in New Zealand, and the kindred spirits of the two.

Yet his connection to the IWW further aided his downfall. Like moths to a flame, Josephs' confiscated material was sent directly to the top of the anti-labour ladder and into the heavy hands of Sir John Salmond—Solicitor-General of New Zealand from 1910–20, author of the War Regulations, and an ardent antisocialist. Salmond spared little effort ensuring that Josephs' mail order activities were stopped short.

However, if Salmond had got his way, Josephs would have suffered much more than mail censorship. The Solicitor-General repeatedly searched for ways to make Josephs' new home a jail cell, either "as a disaffected and dangerous alien under Clause 2 of the War Regulations," or "in the alternative... prosecuted under Clause 4 of the same regulations for distributing or having in his possession for sale... documents inciting violence, lawlessness and disorder."[34] Josephs was only spared from twelve months' imprisonment with hard labour by a technicality—the related War Regulations had only been amended on 20 September 1915, therefore "evidence would have to be acts done after that date." Salmond relented, fearful that "questions might afterwards arise as to whether the military authorities had been justified in taking such a course by the evidence before them."[35]

Instead, Salmond had all of Josephs' mail stopped and suppressed:

the best course in the meantime is to arrange with the Post Office to have all correspondence addressed to Josephs... stopped and examined. It may be that such examination will show that Josephs is an active agent of the IWW or other anarchist and criminal organizations, and that on this evidence steps could be taken either for his prosecution or for his internment.[36]

One such correspondent was his Christchurch comrade Syd Kingsford, who until January 1915 was regularly receiving parcels of anarchist literature from Josephs:

please have enquiries made and report furnished regarding a man named 'Syd Kingsford'... who appears to be an agent in Christchurch for the distribution of anarchist and IWW literature. Search was recently made in Wellington on the premises of Philip Josephs, and it would appear from books found in Josephs' possession that he obtains such literature from America and supplies same to Kingsford.[37]

Two police intelligence reports show that Kingsford was under constant surveillance: "I have to report that Kingsford is a single man of about 25 years of age, a cabinet maker... he is now working with his father at 213 Durham Street and lives at 107 Riccarton Road;" while Chief Censor Colonel Gibbon made sure his correspondence was also censored: "the necessary action has been taken to have correspondence for Josephs and Syd Kingsford censored."[38] Salmond's censorship served its purpose: a 1915 Freedom Press account book notes that the October, November, and December shipments to Josephs were "refused."[39]

Another Wobbly-anarchist under the state's spotlight was J. Sweeney, who in 1915 was working in the backcountry of Blenheim. Sweeny had been an open advocate of the IWW since 1911, when the *Maoriland Worker* published his call for "IWW clubs in the four large centres" to "organize and educate the workers of New Zealand."[40] His letter for Josephs, which contained an order for a year's subscription to *Freedom*, *Mother Earth*, and *The Spur* (and which ended in typical Wobbly flair with "Yours for Direct Action, No Political Dope"), never made it past the censor, who instead forwarded it to Colonel Gibbon so police could find more Wobblies to monitor. "Herewith please receive a letter addressed to the anarchist P. Josephs. I forward it, as you may possibly wish the Police to know who are his correspondents in New Zealand."[41]

The material confiscated from Josephs—and the foreign and international titles in particular—displays the depth of transnational networks he had built up during his years in New Zealand, and suggests a broad target audience for his pamphlets and papers. Similarly, the energy spent on the suppression of Josephs' mail order activities by the state also highlights the influence of anarchist and socialist literature in New Zealand, and hints at a deep fear of its revival. Salmond, and those around him, were determined not to allow dissent of any kind to reach pre-1913 levels. As well as waging a foreign war at the behest of Britain, the New Zealand state had conducted its own home-front harassment—a war on socialism.

CHAPTER 9

LOOSE ENDS

Although those in New Zealand wanting anarchist literature could still order direct from the source (a 1917 raid on the US offices of *Mother Earth* revealed four New Zealand subscribers on the mailing list: Anti-Militarist in Christchurch; S. Edilson of Wellington, one of Josephs' 1911 subscribers; D. Emerson in Hokitika; and the *Maoriland Worker*), and unless Josephs took another name and post box, the targeting of his mail spelled the end of ten years' worth of anarchist agitation via the not-so-private post. With the mainstream press firmly behind the government, public anarchist activity during the later stages of the First World War would almost certainly result in further repression, placing Josephs in a precarious position. Did he risk continuing his anarchist activity in a far-from-fruitful climate (at the certain expense of both him and his family) or lie low for the rest of the war? He had already come agonisingly close to jail time with hard labour and now he was short-listed by Salmond as a prominent subversive—a member of a 'criminal' organization and one to be watched. Being from the Russian empire also complicated matters, for from 1917 onwards, the Russian Revolution and the bogey of the Bolsheviks soon rivalled anarchism as the mainstream media's favourite scapegoats.

In the end, he did not have much of a choice. The safety net put in place by the New Zealand state successfully brought an end to Josephs' anarchist activities. By 1919, he had left Wellington for the rural township of Bunnythorpe, and in 1921 he finally left the country for Australia.

Yet despite wartime censorship and the stifling of anarchist dissent, there are still traces of anarchism being portrayed positively in the public realm at that time. In 1917, *NZ Truth*, a populist paper edited by ex-NZSP member and comrade of Josephs, Robert Hogg, published a series of letters that discussed the ideas of 'the Anarchist Prince' Kropotkin. Using the relatively secure columns of the letters section, Joseph Kidd of Auckland responded in 'Progress or the Servile State' to what he believed was a "rather long-drawn out" discussion on spiritualism. "Abstract ideas like Spiritualism may be very interesting to some people, but, to my mind, the first consideration of every intelligent man and woman is the coming conflict between capitalism and labour; that is to say, between useful workers and parasites." He had listened to "every shade of opinion one could possibly hear outside (and perhaps inside) a mental hospital," but found that Kropotkin had "the clearest summing up of things":

> Kropotkin says: 'The people commit blunders or blunder when they have to choose by ballot some hair-brained candidate who solicits the honour of representing them, and takes upon himself to know all, to do all, and to organize all. But when they (the people) take upon themselves to organize what they know, what touches them directly, they do it better than all the 'talking shops' put together.'[1]

In a reply titled 'Parliamentarism Deplored,' a writer from Te Awamutu with the pen name 'Conquest of Bread' heartily endorsed Joseph Kidd and the anarchist communism of Kropotkin (although not surprisingly, both letters are careful not to mention the term). "Society (or the toiling portion of it, and they are the only ones who count), have tried every kind of representation" states the writer, "and the experience has been ghastly and gruesome. Failure is writ large upon the experiment of leaving to plausible individuals the carrying out of social functions—functions that should have been directly initiated and administered by the toilers themselves." After quoting from Kropotkin's influential work, *The Conquest of Bread*, the anonymous author finished by urging:

> all those who are not mentally suffused with dependence upon the virus of political delusion (ballots or representation) to get busy and by careful preparation (education) and organization (industrial) to so fit themselves and be able to teach others, that the coming changes in society do not catch them napping. All dependence upon political aspirants or incumbents must be cast to the winds; they must visualize

a state of society, where the individual reigns supreme, where each harms not the other, consequently being no need for laws.[2]

The tone of the letter is remarkably similar to that used by Josephs in his own writings. If the author was not Josephs in disguise, then alternatively, it was from another New Zealand anarchist with an effective employment of English and a clear understanding of Kropotkin's anarchism.

Indeed, Kropotkin seems to have been favoured by Hogg and *NZ Truth* at that time. With a literary play on a well-known (and in this case alliterative) Maori term of approbation, an article titled 'Kropotkin Kapai!' announced: "we are glad to have news of Prince Peter Kropotkin! According to the following which appeared in London 'Justice' (anti-Bolshevik) of March 20 last, the great Russian is well."[3] A double-column, page-length letter from Kropotkin denouncing Bolshevism as "the dictatorship of one party" whose inherent evils had "been increased by war conditions" was also republished in October 1920, and included Kropotkin's famous statement: "this is the way NOT to accomplish the Revolution."[4] *NZ Truth* even published a lengthy account of Kropotkin's funeral taken from *Freedom*, which included details about the repression of anarchists by the Bolshevik regime.[5]

What was Josephs' reaction to Bolshevism and the Revolution that had taken place in the lands he had once called home? Was he swayed (like a large number of anarchists) by what, at the time, seemed like a sweeping social revolution, aided in part by the Bolshevik's idea of the dictatorship of the proletariat? Or was he among those anarchists who, although they supported the workers' soviets and the libertarian nature of their struggle, came to the conclusion that the Bolshevist regime simply fulfilled the traditional anarchist prophecies of orthodox Marxism and the pitfalls of political seizures of power? Likewise, what was Josephs' reaction to Kropotkin's support of the Allies during the First World War? It is evident from Josephs' correspondence and acts of solidarity with Russian revolutionaries that Russia was never far from his mind, and that Kropotkin played an influential part on his politics. Kropotkin was by far Josephs' most stocked author, and that the Wellington anarchist collective was called Freedom Group also illustrates Josephs' indebtedness to Kropotkin and his association with Freedom Press. Yet, due to the frustrating lack of records, we may never know what he made of the international anarchist debates on Bolshevism, and Kropotkin's stance during the First World War.

The later years of Josephs' life are also lacking in source material, but when the facts are compared with his earlier activities, they seem rather… well, normal. Prebble posits the possibility of Josephs returning to Russia after the 1917 Revolution, and that a man under surveillance in the 1920s named G. Solomon could have been Josephs. What we do know is that Josephs continued to run his tailor shop at 95 Cuba Street until December 1916, when he swapped suits for overalls and gumboots—the family having left the city for rural Bunnythorpe (about 150 kilometres north). In 1918 and 1919 street directories, Josephs was listed as a farmer, and with Sophia, he opened a bank account at the Sanson-Bulls branch of the Bank of New Zealand, listing his occupation as 'Grocer.' Their oldest daughter Jeanie used to recount stories to her children of filling hefty pails of milk most mornings, fresh from the family cow.

Whether Josephs continued his mail order activities from his new address in rural New Zealand is unknown. The censorship file at Archives New Zealand contains no other confiscated mail after 1915 except for one tantalising item, a February 1919 edition of the Australian communist paper *Knowledge and Unity*. Was it sent by an old anarchist comrade, now a member of the Communist Party of Australia, who did not know Josephs had left Wellington years earlier? Or perhaps Josephs, who was preparing to return to Wellington, was testing whether his mailbox was still monitored? Evidently it was, for the paper was stopped, suppressed, and filed by the censor.

After a brief taste of country life, and in an uneasy truce with the state, Josephs was back in Wellington in September 1920. He was also back in business—the manager of the Crown Tea Rooms that, according to his adverts in the *Maoriland Worker*, was a late-night tuck shop opposite Parliament House specializing in hot pies.[6] In an ironic twist, Josephs—the most surveilled anarchist during the First World War—spent his last days in New Zealand selling pies outside parliament.

Less mysterious is the surveillance of G. Solomon, who was in fact his friend Solomon Gordon. Having been born in Russia, associating with anarchists such as Josephs, and being a prominent figure in labour circles, ensured Solomon was also under state scrutiny. As Goldman in *The History of The Jews in New Zealand* writes, "in the home of the

Gordons, the leaders of the warring [social democrat] factions frequently met... agreement was finally reached, resulting in the formation of the New Zealand Labour Party in July, 1916."[7] That year Josephs had shared his tailor shop at 95 Cuba Street with Gordon, and it is entirely possible that he could have been an anarchist fly on the wall during these discussions.

For Josephs, the choice to leave New Zealand and its stifling political surroundings may not have been a hard one. Thanks to a 1920 letter to *Freedom* by an anarchist named Bert Olds, we are given an interesting perspective of New Zealand conditions during the last years of Josephs' stay. "In New Zealand we are just beginning to feel the real pinch," wrote Olds:

> the cost of living is beyond all expectations, and is going to make itself felt before this year dies. Boots in 1914 costing 25s. now cost 70s.; suits, tailor-made, 90s., are now 260s.; and bread is up to 1s. per loaf... on the head of everyone of us is a debt of £250. Just think of it, New Zealand is larger than the British Isles, and every bit as rich in mines and soil; and yet its small population have their noses to the emery stone.[8]

While wages rose slightly, "the workers do not see yet that they cannot catch up to the cost of living," and thanks to the "big bluff" of craft unionism and the "political dope" of the newly formed Labour Party, "Labour men in New Zealand are impossible from an Anarchist point of view... they won't think beyond their own noses."[9]

It seems Josephs quit the country while he was ahead. After an eventful life lived in Wellington, the Josephs family (like the Gordons) soon settled down in Sydney, where Philip opened another shop and continued to work as a tailor. In his rooms on Pitt Street, Sydney, grandchildren would play with his book of fabric samples while Josephs was hard at work, complaining that the electric sewing machine a salesman had lent him was too slow for his liking.

While his work did not change pace, it appears he left his anarchist activity to days past. No stirrings of subversion in Sydney have come to light, although it seems he kept in touch with his kiwi comrades. His family remember one visit from a New Zealand friend who, at the age of sixty-five and having some money, was cruising the world with abandon, believing himself to be close to the final curtain. Instead, he died in his nineties—penniless but rich in experience.

For Josephs, time ran out faster than his friend. At sixty-nine years of age the well-liked, gentle, and humorous grandparent—and the mainstay of early anarchism in New Zealand—lost the age-old struggle against fate, and died of a heart attack on 25 April 1946.

Meanwhile, back in New Zealand, a syndicalist upsurge culminating in the 1951 Lockout of the militant Watersiders' Union was about to erupt. Although far from an anarchist organization, the principles of direct action, industrial organization, working class counter-culture, and solidarity—principles for which Josephs and the throng of other revolutionary syndicalists had fought bitterly—played a major part in the watersiders' weaponry.[10] Even the odd Wobbly was involved.[11] Their struggle for economic freedom, and the fights that followed, pay tribute to the work done forty years earlier. The seeds of revolutionary struggle that Josephs, as an anarchist communist, had helped to plant in New Zealand during the early twentieth century were still visible. Indeed, they have a tendency to sprout whenever the conditions are ripe.

EPILOGUE

A definitive history is, in any case, a dream. In the end, one can only work toward that goal in the hope of filling in a few of the blanks; and perhaps creating new interest in filling in those that remain.[1]

Although this modest account of New Zealand anarchism before 1921 focuses primarily on Philip Josephs and those who left traces of their activities behind, it is entirely possible (indeed, highly likely) that many others in New Zealand identified as anarchist and agitated as such, but are lost to history because no documentation survives. This is particularly pertinent in terms of New Zealand anarchism that—denounced by parliament, from the pulpit, and in the press—was always a precarious and minority position. Unfortunately, the true scope of early anarchism in New Zealand may never be known.

History has also been unkind when it comes to women and the far left. Apart from Lola Ridge, I have not been able to find other examples of female anarchists in New Zealand. There were women in the NZSP (such as Mrs. Wilson), and the IWW had at least two active female members: "a certain Mrs. Chapman was the newspaper commission agent in 1913," writes Moriarty-Patten, while Lila Freeman (who later married prominent New Zealand communist, Andy Barras) was also an "active participant in the struggle."[2] Was 'Grandma Green'—the "grand old woman of the revolutionary movement" who spread "the gospel of education towards revolution" in Huntly and who formed a women's socialist league for that purpose—an anarchist?[3] What about Sophia Josephs and other companeras, whose domestic and support work was the foundation of their partner's political activity? Did they share their sweetheart's politics? The answers to such questions await the keen researcher.[4]

Despite the lack of historical records it is clear anarchism in New Zealand has a legacy that can date back to 1904, if not earlier, thanks to the personal perseverance of Josephs and others like him. Its development was fragmented—typified by the decentralized activity of various anarchists placed in their immediate socialist milieu—which, besides making historical research difficult, partly explains an "anarchist influence without any apparent strong organization at the centre of it."[5] However, this fragmented and decentralized anarchist influence does not fit the traditional labour history measures of success. A focus on structural or organizational forms, and membership figures, betrays any social and cultural impact anarchism had on the New Zealand labour movement. As Salvatore Salerno writes, social and cultural activity is often occluded by an emphasis on a structural, economic and institutional form, and therefore overshadows the links "between working class culture, politics, and social formations."[6]

As an influential propagandist for working-class struggle, Josephs' involvement in the NZSP and the working-class counter-culture of Wellington—his economic classes, street meetings, and public lectures, the radical space that was his tailor shop, and the distribution of revolutionary reading material—contributed to a radical community and culture much bigger than himself or the membership count of the Freedom Group. The exact influence of New Zealand anarchism in cultural and discursive terms is difficult to measure. Yet it could be argued that the anarchist movement in New Zealand was larger than previously recognized—its philosophy of direct action and class solidarity "broader and more complex than the concern with formal organizational criteria."[7]

There is no doubt that the activity of Josephs, and the various individuals across the country who identified as anarchists, form but a small part of the revolutionary upsurge that was the pre-1920 period. Anarchists were always in the minority and failed to spark any mass movement in explicitly anarchist terms. Yet Josephs' activity, and the actions of other anarchists like him, surely had a hand in the normalization of syndicalist tactics and the ideology of direct action—an ideology that crystallized into one of New Zealand's most fraught and revolutionary periods. Josephs' transnational diffusion of anarchist doctrine, his links to the wider anarchist movement, and his involvement with Freedom Press (through the distribution of their anarchist politics), ensured anarchist ideas and tactics received a hearing in the New Zealand labour movement well beyond its minority status. Despite Olssen's suggestion that "few rank and file revolutionaries had much knowledge of syndicalist and anarchist ideology," it is clear that anarchism—alongside other shades of socialist thought—contributed to the militancy of the movement on a scale not readily recognized by most historical accounts.[8] Likewise, Josephs' activity places him, and New Zealand anarchism, firmly on the global anarchist map. While the Auckland group and the Wellington Freedom Group was no Federación Anarquista Ibérica (Iberian Anarchist Federation), the fact that anarchists came together, formed collectives, and propagated the principles of anarchism, at the very least, deserves remembering.[9]

By illuminating the recorded activity of anarchists in New Zealand during the early years of the twentieth century, I hope that the relative absence of anarchism in the annals of New Zealand labour historiography can be rectified—even if this anarchist activity never grew beyond a minority movement of a few individuals, or was limited to the lingering effects of a cultural conveying of class feeling. This absence is magnified by a number of historians who, in emphasising the conclusions of some labour leaders after the 1912 and 1913 Strikes—that industrial action alone was not enough to bring about socialism, and therefore the site of struggle should shift from the workplace to the benches of parliament—view everything prior to the 1935 Labour government's parliamentary election as its "pre-history."[10] According to such a narrative, "notions of transforming society and advancing the cause of the working class by combining revolutionary politics and industrial action were tested and found to be wanting."[11]

While it is true parliamentary socialism gathered its forces and became the majority position, it does not illustrate the whole picture— indeed, it negates and discredits the anarchist or revolutionary syndicalist position and its politics of direct action. However, according to Taylor, "obituaries of the revolutionary movement, whether written by various actors in 1913 or subsequently by historians, were premature. There was dissent from [the Labourist] consensus before, during, and after the strike."[12] As Olssen himself points out, the class struggle of 1908–1913 deeply affected New Zealand workers: "the new popularity of the stop-work meeting, the sympathy and the wildcat strike... and the popularity of new symbols and slogans of class show this clearly."[13]

The Great Strike of 1913 played a major part in raising the rank-and-file's awareness of self-activity and the power of collective action outside of strike action. This did not end in 1913. For example, in order to win concessions on the job, go-slows actually increased after the Great Strike. Well into 1919, newspapers were dismayed that workers were slowing down production, and direct action on the job (rather than simply walking out on strike) became a much-used tactic in the revolutionary toolbox.[14] Work-to-rule action on New Zealand wharves and by miners against conscription, and the formation of organizations like the Alliance of Labour in 1919 and the One Big Union Movement in 1920, suggests a second wave of syndicalism and allows for an alternative to the Labourist position that posits a preference for parliamentary politics.[15] This alternative would not have been possible were it not for anarchists and syndicalists like Philip Josephs.

Instead, a much livelier and revolutionary line can be traced from Josephs and the upsurge of anti-parliamentary politics, to the various struggles throughout New Zealand's history that have aimed to go beyond the limitations of state forms. At the time of printing, New Zealand has a number of both formal and informal regional anarchist collectives, national organizations, radical bookstores and social centres across the country, an anarchist publishing house, and various anarchist-inspired intentional communities. Unfortunately, the same techniques used by those in power to discredit such forms in the past have continued throughout the years. Anarchists—whether in New Zealand or around the world—are still painted universally by the media as anti-social extremists who are not averse to violence and terror. Indeed, a quick scan of any modern newspaper is like re-opening the pages of the 1907 daily that decried anarchism as a bomb-wielding philosophy. An alternative account, one that considers the everyday activity of anarchists like Josephs, can go some way in countering this stereotype, placing the anarchist's activity back in the realm of reality.

Although we live in totally different times, and although past examples should not (and cannot) be replicated, we still gain important insights that help place our present situation in context. Considering the current conditions of capitalism that, in a sense, seem to have come full circle—with its casualization of labour, extension of the working day and the complete subsumption of life to capital, and its ineffectual union organizations—Josephs' anarchist activity and the syndicalist surge of the early twentieth century serve as pertinent reminders of the successes (and failures) of New Zealand's revolutionary movement. Therefore, if history is to be more than a nostalgic stroll through the past, and if the historian's responsibility "is to find those social processes and structures which promise an alternative to the ones now dominant,"[16] then historical awareness should serve as "a key reminder that we still live in a society deeply divided by class. The actions of the past stand as inspiring, yet unfinished movements."[17]

APPENDICES

TRADES UNIONISM IN NEW ZEALAND: IS IT A FAILURE?

Philip Josephs
Commonweal, January 1907

When we look back through the pages of history and mark the development of industrial organizations, we find in every country the lower wage-slaves had to go through a tremendous struggle to wring from their exploiters the right of combination. We find ever and anon some one of the Workers, more intelligent and more brave than his fellows, standing forth and exhorting them to unite against the tyranny of their masters. At first no punishment was too excessive for such agitators. One would be cast into a dungeon to pine and die in darkness; another found himself tied to the tail-end of a cart and dragged along the public streets, to the amusement of the unthinking; another, still more outspoken mayhap than the rest, would be tortured and burned at the stake as a conspirator against society. Still the number of courageous men continued to grow, and at last the wage-slaves heard and understood the message, but not before hundreds, ay, thousands, had died behind cruel prison walls, or laid down their lives on the scaffold and the guillotine in the great struggle for freedom. The history of Trades Unionism is full of bloody pages concerning the Workers' fight against oppression. It isn't very long since even in Britain if a Worker expressed himself in favour of organizing the Working Class, he was at once arrested and sentenced to a long term of imprisonment with hard labour.

The early object of Trades Unionism was not only to secure higher wages and shorter hours, but to protect its members from social and political danger. As the struggle proceeded Trades Unionism grew in strength, and its leaders grew influential and powerful. Many of these, especially in more recent days, lost sight of the true principle on which their organizations were based and led the unions aside after mere will-o'-the-wisps. In time the cardinal principles became so obscured that instead of union standing by union we find them often fighting each other at the behest of their leaders and, we may be sure, to the advantage of the employers. And further, time and time again these same leaders in times of stress were bribed by the employing classes to cunningly betray their fellows. So oft did this occur that all leaders were suspected and jealously watched, and if one showed the slightest inclination of favouring the employers at the expense of the unions he was immediately expelled from the movement.

Subsequently a further development took place, and some of the Workers determined not only to better their conditions as regards wages and hours of labour, but to organize with a view to overthrowing the whole system of exploitation which holds them in bondage and subjection, and establishing a system of society based on fraternity, justice, and liberty. They held that Trades Unions were not chiefly to concern themselves with discussing petty reforms, but to teach the Workers to realise the existence of the Class War in present day society, that their interests as a class were to be pitted against another class—whose every action was dictated by a desire to rule and exploit the proletariat.

Modern trades unionism may be defined as follows: An organization of Workers voluntarily combined to protect the interests of its members economically and socially, and ready at any moment to protest by word, and if need be, by deed against any wrong which may be inflicted, or attempted to be inflicted, on its members by their employers; to seek the betterment of the Workers' conditions of labour, and to aim at the final overthrow of commercial capitalism, and the replacing it with a system of industrial organization in which every unit of society physically and mentally fit, will have an equal opportunity to join in the production of wealth, and that all who make use of such equal opportunity shall have the right to that portion of wealth accruing from their labour. Their will be no more industrial competition, no more exploitation, and misery and poverty will be forgotten in the joys of fellowship and good cheer which shall be the equal portion of all the Workers of the Commonweal.

Trades Unionism in New Zealand had not to pass through the same hard and bitter struggle which beset its development in other countries.

Immigrants brought the methods and regulations of Trades Unions with which they were familiar at Home, thus recognising the fact that the economic struggle was worldwide. Correspondence was opened up with the Old World Trades Unions, advanced literature and newspapers were imported and eagerly read by the more active and earnest members, thus keeping them well informed of the line of march of the Workers of the World. The majority of the Workers, however, in time became careless and indifferent. Times were good, their wages and conditions were fair—and decidedly better than in the lands of their birth, and Trades Unionism in New Zealand languished. In 1890, the year of the great maritime strike, the awakening came, and the Workers were forced to array themselves in the order of battle against the common enemy. The principle of the Class Struggle was recognized—but partially it is true—and the Workers learned that their interests and their employers interests were not the same. The result of the 1890 struggle banded the Workers of New Zealand together, and much good work was accomplished during the subsequent two or three years. Then the old enemy—political differences—intervened. Interested parties succeeded in dividing the ranks on imaginary differences and non-essentials, and Unionism at the present time exists only for the benefit of a few salaried officers. Not 30 per cent of the Workers in any trade are Unionists, and less than five per cent of these take any live interest in the affairs of their unions. And what are the subjects discussed at these meetings? Is the objective of Trades Unionism ever mentioned or inculcated in the speeches of their leaders? And on election day do they march in a body as Trades Unionists (as they do on Labour Day) and vote as Trades Unionists? I'm afraid the answer to these questions must be unsatisfactory, and the fact admitted that Trades Unionism in New Zealand is reactionary, disorganized, and almost non-existent.

After the maritime strike, already referred to (which failed because of the want of organization), the Conciliation Board and Arbitration Court were set up. In these the exploiter and the exploited meet and mutually arrange the amount of exploitation which satisfied the rapaciousness of the former, and to which the latter will submit and still manage to exist and propagate his species! Did I not live in New Zealand I should scout the idea as outwith the sphere of possibility. The Conciliation Board and Arbitration Act has dealt Trades Unionism in New Zealand its death blow. The conditions of labour and wages paid are now decided, not by the votes of the members of the unions, but by an outside tribunal, two-thirds of the members of which are in no way under the control of the unions. From its very constitution what could the Workers expect but that of the interests of their employers would be first and paramount every time. The Workers have been robbed of their fighting weapon, the Strike. The enthusiasm of the members of the unions has been killed, and all interest in Trades Unionism has gone by the board. The Union meeting is a place for transacting routine business only, instead of a rendezvous of the advanced guard of progress and a school of preparation for the great coming event—the Social Revolution.

THE GENERAL STRIKE AS A WEAPON AGAINST CONSCRIPTION

Philip Josephs
Maoriland Worker, 18 August 1911

Everyone seems to be at present more or less interested in the Compulsory Military Act.

One section of the community, probably constituting the largest, are in favour of this act; another section seems to be divided on the matter—some are in favour of it, and some are rather desirous of an organized citizen army. There is also still another section in the community who recognizes no quarrel with people of other countries, because economic conditions being universally identical, find a compulsory or citizen army not only useless but dangerous.

To show the justifications of those sections or parties, it is necessary to distinguish them from each other for the purpose of analysis. The first section constitutes the Liberal and Conservative Party, the second section the trade unions and Labour Party, the third section the Socialist Party.

The first section, or party, say that we have to protect our interests and liberties from foreign invasion. I can quite understand their arguments and their demands for compulsory military training. The land owners, big farmers, manufacturers, and large storekeepers own 95% of the nation's wealth; it is therefore in their interest to have a well trained army prepared to protect their interests from foreign invasion;

consequently they try to compel everyone to abide by this law, whether they believe it to be right or not; those who disobey the law are either to be fined or put in gaol. From such evidence, we may logically conclude that this particular section, who are so interested in compelling people to obey the law, are certainly that section who monopolised the nation's wealth, and thereby denied the masses of their original rights to the wealth they created. The reason why this sector have such a great following is because they have the press and the religious institutions on their side, the press continually trying to show its readers the benefits of this Act. The press, having an enormous influence on the people, these form their opinions accordingly, and are ready to defend those who really are their greatest enemies.

The second section, who constitute a large number of the workers, and also call themselves the most advanced section in society, always promise the people the very best they can achieve. Of course they must have a citizen army. Their reasons for that desire are partially similar to that of the first section; they are trying to convince us that we have certain rights and liberties other nations have not got—therefore, they require an army to protect these rights from foreign invasion. In order to discover whether their desires are right or wrong, it is necessary first of all to look at what liberties the people really have. They never forget to tell the people at every opportunity how they are continually robbed of their rights by their employers, their landlords, by the monopolist, by speculators—all trying to rob the wealth and rights of the workers. There is consequently nothing whatever left for the worker, and therefore he has nothing to defend, and even a citizen army is quite useless for him. The depravation of the workers' wealth and rights exist in every country alike. Our enemies are not abroad. They exist in our midst. We should not try and oppose them but combine with them for one purpose, namely, to fight those who really rob us both of our wealth, instead of opposing or shooting down (as the case may be) those who have never done us any harm. Their argument in favour of a citizen army is without foundation or insincere, even according to their own assertions.

The third section is the Socialist Party. They certainly oppose the Act directly right out. They refuse to obey the laws that are made against their wish, and without their consent. They say that the people have not been consulted on the question of compulsory military training, and they demand the immediate repeal of this pernicious Act. I may say frankly it does not matter whether there are laws in favour of it or not—laws were always made for the protection of one class against another, even if the laws were made by a Labour Party or Socialist Party. If it is dangerous for one section to make laws against another, would it not similarly apply to either one of those sections referred to above? The Socialist Party believes that all the present institutions are fundamentally corrupt. In order to realise their Socialist ideal, it is necessary to outroot these foundations to enable them to put a strong foundation in its place. Why the present institutions are corrupt, is because they assisted to frame and uphold the present laws, which are certainly against the general welfare of the people. The Socialist Party, being against such laws that are made in favour of one class to oppress another, cannot conscientiously use legal means in opposing such laws; it would be like stretching a piece of elastic that goes back with tremendous reactionary force. We must once and for all realise that the workers must find means independent of those in accordance with the existing laws, knowing the laws always have worked against them.

Where are the industrial unions? Especially the Federation of Labor? Where are the miners of New Zealand, who have always showed such heroism in their brave fights against their masters and the present society in general? I believe the miners, who are industrially organized, with the assistance of the Federation of Labor, should declare a general strike as a protest against compulsory military training. I am confident that within a week the Act will be repealed. They have already realised their strength and influence—why not use it in this case effectively.

Many will say such actions would be too harsh. What have the Government done by passing such an Act? The Government have ignored you. They forced conscription on you suddenly, and if they have the right to commit such a harsh act, it is also right for the workers to do exactly as their opponents have done to them.

The question arises: Are you going to allow your children to be imprisoned for disobeying this Act? It would be the greatest crime for you not to show a greater protest than you are presently showing. The meetings held to protest against the Act are a little too respectable. Nothing will be gained by such methods. You want to show your direct great power against the governing classes, in order to make them realise the danger in passing such laws in the future.

LIST OF BOOKS AND PAPERS FOUND
IN PHILIP JOSEPHS' POSSESION

"Report of Detective-Sergeant James McIlveney," 12 October 1915.

The Place of Anarchism in Socialistic Evolution
Erskine on the Limits of Toleration
Militarism and Revolution
Freedom Pamphlets
Liberal Opponents and Conservative Friends
The Last War
Modern Science and Anarchism
The Iron Heel
Trade Unionism and Anarchism
International Socialist Review
Unabridged Freedom of Speech
Our Vanishing Liberty of the Press
John Bull's Other Island
The Martyrdom of Berkman
The Martyrdom of Ferrer
The Logic and Economics of the Class Struggle
Industrial Unionism
The Basis of Trade Unionism
The Repeal
The Tragic Story of the Waihi Strike
Chunks of IWWism
Revolution and the IWW
The Defence Act and Criticism
Direct Action versus Legislation
The Law of Nature and Natural Rights
The Socialist Platform
The New International Review
Problems and Perils of Socialism
The Capitalist Class
Evolution and Revolution
Why
The Defense of Free Speech
The Labour Unrest

The Civil Service Socialist
The Wage System
Anarchism
The Great Illusion
Land and Liberty
The Kingdom of God and Socialism
The Logic of the Machine
Fifteen Questions
Facts v. Fiction
A Vindication of Natural Society
Anarchism and Malthus
The Struggle for Existence
Impressions
Industrial Problems
A Critical Examination of Socialism
Syndicalism and Labour
Pages of Socialist History
Clue to the Economic Labyrinth
Questions for a Reformed Parliament
Theosophy and Social Reconstruction
The Bennett—Mills Debate on the Unity Scheme
Kropotkin—The Man and his Message
War
Brotherhood
Francisco Ferrer—His life work and Martyrdom
Social General Strike
The Positivist Review
Anarchism in Socialistic Evolution
The International Anarchist Congress
Anarchism and American Traditions
Responsibility and Solidarity
Fire and Revolution
The Anti-Conscription League
Workingmen don't vote
The Workers University Direct Action Group
Library of Anarchism
The Extinction of Mankind

Preamble and Constitution of the Industrial Workers of the World
Large number of Labour newspapers and News Bulletins
Syndicalism
Mother Earth
The Anarchist Revolution
40 magazines and books in foreign print
11 newspapers in foreign print
Chinese magazine
Chinese Anarchist circular
Account book
Contribution book

ENDNOTES

INTRODUCTION

1. *Evening Post*, 7 May 1906.
2. G.K. Chesterton's *The Man Who Was Thursday* is a metaphysical thriller set amongst anarchist cells, police spies, and wicked plots of subversion. His far from sympathetic portrayal of anarchism in novel form was one of the earliest, and unfortunately, the most enduring. J.W. Arrowsmith Publishing, 1908.
3. Daniel Guerin, as cited by David Berry, *A History of the French Anarchist Movement: 1917 to 1945*, AK Press, 2009, p. 15.
4. Vadim Damier, *Anarcho-Syndicalism in the 20th Century*, Black Cat Press, 2009, p. 3.
5. *Marlborough Express*, 16 November 1907.
6. Kerry Taylor, "Workers Vanguard or People's Voice?: the Communist Party of New Zealand from Origins to 1946," Thesis, Victoria University of Wellington, 1994, p. 7.
7. Frank Prebble, *"Troublemakers" Anarchism and Syndicalism: The Early Years of the Libertarian Movement in Aotearoa/New Zealand*, Libertarian Press, 1995.
8. Rob Knowles, *Political Economy From Below: Economic Thought in Communitarian Anarchism, 1840–1914*, Routledge, 2004, p. 5.
9. Steven Hirsch & Lucien van der Walt, "Rethinking Anarchism, Syndicalism, the Colonial and Postcolonial Experience" in Steven Hirsch & Lucien van der Walt (eds.), *Anarchism and Syndicalism in the Colonial and Postcolonial World, 1870–1940: The Praxis of National Liberation, Internationalism, and Social Revolution*, Brill, 2011.
10. Ibid., p. ii.
11. Prebble, *"Troublemakers"*; Constance Bantman, "The Militant Go-between: Emile Pouget's Transnational Propaganda (1880–1914)" in *Labour History Review*, 74(3), 2009, p. 274–287; David Berry & Constance Bantman (eds.), *New Perspectives on Anarchism, Labour and Syndicalism: The Individual, the National and the Transnational*, Cambridge Scholars Publishing, 2010; Marcel van der Linden, *Transnational Labour History: Explorations*, Ashgate, 2003.
12. Michael Schmidt & Lucien van der Walt, *Black Flame: The Revolutionary Class Politics of Anarchism and Syndicalism*, AK Press, 2009, p. 71.
13. Eric Olssen, email to the author, 20 August 2010.
14. Schmidt & van der Walt, *Black Flame*. The New Zealand Federation of Labor (FOL) was a syndicalist-inspired organization that had a large influence on the New Zealand labour movement (see p. 66).
15. Hirsch & van der Walt, "Rethinking Anarchism," p. iiv.

1. RISING EXPECTATIONS AND DASHED HOPES

1. "Josephs, P-Naturalisation Certificate," National Archives of Australia: A1, 1926/3885.
2. Nicholas J. Evans, "The Port Jews of Libau, 1880–1914" in *Jewish Culture and History*, 7(7.2), p. 201.
3. Ibid., p. 200.
4. Ibid., p. 201.
5. Nathan A. Ro'ia, "Liepaja," *YIVO Encyclopedia of Jews in Eastern Europe*, available online at http://www.yivoencyclopedia.org/article.aspx/Liepaja.
6. Henry Tobias, *The Jewish Bund in Russia: From Its Origins to 1905*, Stanford University Press, 1972, p. 27.
7. Leo Errera, *The Russian Jews: Extermination or Emancipation?*, David Nutt, London, 1894, p. 46.
8. Paul Avrich, *The Russian Anarchists*, WW Norton & Co, 1978, p. 9.
9. Martin A. Miller, *Kropotkin*, University of Chicago Press, 1976, p. 200.
10. Tobias, *The Jewish Bund in Russia*, p. 9.
11. Josifs Steimanis, *History of Latvian Jews*, Columbia University Press-East European Monographs, 2002, p. 79.
12. Avrich, *The Russian Anarchists*, p. 18.
13. Ibid.
14. Ibid.
15. Ibid., p. 12.
16. Philip Ruff, email to the author, 7 November 2010.
17. Kenneth Collins, *Second City Jewry: The Jews of Glasgow in the Age of Expansion 1790–1919*, Scottish Jewish Archives, 1990, p. 45.
18. William J. Fishman, *East End Jewish Radicals 1875–1914*, Duckworth, 1974, p. 18.
19. Avrich, *The Russian Anarchists*, p. 16.
20. Salo W. Baron, *The Russian Jew Under Tsars and Soviets*, Macmillan Publishing, 1976, p. 49.
21. Evans, "The Port Jews of Libau,," p. 207.
22. Fishman, *East End Jewish Radicals*, p. 38.
23. Evans, "The Port Jews of Libau," p. 206.

2. GLASGOW AND THE ANARCHISTS

1. Collins, *Second City Jewry*, p. 45.
2. William Kenefick, "Jewish and Catholic Irish Relations: The Glasgow Waterfront c.1880–1914" in David Cesarani & Gemma Romain (eds.), *Jews and Port Cities 1590–1990: Commerce, Community and Cosmopolitanism*, Vallentine Mitchell, 2006, p. 215.
3. Collins, *Second City Jewry*, p. 69.
4. Caroline Josephs, email to the author, 1 February 2012.
5. Collins, *Second City Jewry*, p. 63.
6. Philip and Sophia's children were Jeanie (1898), Fanny (1899), Jessie (1901), Rose (1902), Lulu (1904), Albert (1906), Harold, (1909), and Edie (1913).
7. Peter Fyfe, *Backlands and their Inhabitants*, 1901, p. 15, as cited in Collins, *Second City Jewry*.
8. Collins, *Second City Jewry*, p. 11.
9. Fishman, *East End Jewish Radicals*, p. 42.
10. Ibid., p. 43.

11. Rudolf Rocker, *The London Years*, Five Leaves Press, 2005, pp. 89–90.
12. Fishman, *East End Jewish Radicals*, p. 58.
13. Ibid., p. 57.
14. Ibid., p. 50.
15. Terri Marquez, email to the author, 25 June 2011; Kenefick, *Red Scotland! The Rise and Fall of the Radical Left, c. 1872 to 1932*, Edinburgh University Press, 2007, p. 80.
16. Collins, *Second City Jewry*; Kenefick, "Jewish and Catholic Irish Relations," p. 230.
17. Kenefick, "Jewish and Catholic Irish Relations," p. 230.
18. Emma Goldman, as cited by Peggy Kornegger, "Anarchism: The Feminist Connection" in *Second Wave: a magazine of the new feminism*, 1975.
19. Jesse Cohn, "Messianic Troublemakers: The Past and Present Jewish Anarchism," available online at http://www.zeek.net/politics_0504.shtml.
20. Mairtin O'Cathain, "With a Bent Elbow and a Clenched Fist: A Brief History of the Glasgow Anarchists," available online at http://libcom.org/history/birth-glasgow-anarchism
21. Blair Smith, *Anarchist*, 18 March 1894, as cited by John Quail, *The Slow Burning Fuse: The Lost History of the British Anarchists*, Paladin, 1978, p. 192.
22. Quail, *The Slow Burning Fuse*, p. 240.
23. O'Cathain, "With a Bent Elbow and a Clenched Fist".
24. Rocker, *The London Years*, p. 68.
25. Fishman, *East End Jewish Radicals*, p. 199.
26. Paul Avrich, *Anarchist Voices: An Oral History of Anarchism in America*, Princeton University Press, 1995, p. 173.
27. Cohn, "Messianic Troublemakers," p. 2.
28. Avrich, *Anarchist Voices*, p. 173.
29. Ibid., p. 171.
30. Jesse Cohn, "Anarchy in Yiddish: Famous Jewish Anarchists from Emma Goldman to Noam Chomsky," available online at http://raforum.info/spip.php?article488.
31. Ibid.
32. Collins, *Second City Jewry*, p. 216; Rocker, *The London Years*, p. 80.
33. Rocker, *The London Years*, p. 127.
34. Ivy Raff, email to author, 22 March 2011.

3. A WORKINGMAN'S PARADISE?

1. Georges Fontenis, as cited by Berry, *A History of the French Anarchist Movement*, p. 15.
2. Herbert Roth, *Trade Unions in New Zealand: Past and Present*, Reed Education, 1973, p. 10.
3. Miles Fairburn, *The Ideal Society and its Enemies: The Foundations of Modern New Zealand Society 1850–1900*, Auckland University Press, 1989, p. 22.
4. Ibid.
5. W.H. Oliver, "Rees, Sinclair and the Social Patern," in Peter Munz, (ed.), *The Feel of Truth: Essays in New Zealand and Pacific History*, A.H. Reed, 1969, p. 163.
6. Stuart Moriarty-Patten, "A World to Win, a Hell to Lose: The Industrial Workers of the World in Early Twentieth Century New Zealand," Thesis, Massey University, 2012, p. 6, p. 117.
7. Harry Cleaver, "An Interview with Harry Cleaver," available online at http://libcom.org/library/interview-cleaver.

8. W.B. Sutch, *The Quest For Security in New Zealand 1840 to 1966*, Oxford University Press, 1966, p. 8.

9. Bert Roth & Jenny Hammond, *Toil and Trouble: The Struggle For a Better Life in New Zealand*, Methuen, 1981, p. 10; Keith Sinclair, *A History of New Zealand*, Penguin, 2000 Edition, p. 158.

10. Sutch, *The Quest For Security in New Zealand*, p. ix.

11. Roth & Hammond, *Toil and Trouble*, p. 12–14; Sinclair, *A History of New Zealand*, p. 168.

12. Moriarty-Patten, "A World to Win," p. 6.

13. Steven Eldred-Grigg, *New Zealand Working People 1890–1990*, Dunmore Press, 1990.

14. Melanie Nolan, "Family and Culture: Jack and Maggie McCullough and the Christchurch Skilled Working Class, 1880s–1920s" in John Martin & Kerry Taylor, (eds.), *Culture and the Labour Movement: Essays in New Zealand Labour History*, Dunmore Press, 1991, p. 165.

15. Sinclair, *A History of New Zealand*, p. 209.

16. Peter Clayworth, email to the author, 18 March 2012.

17. Ibid.

18. Eldred-Grigg, *New Zealand Working People*, p. 113.

19. Ibid., p. 112.

20. *New Zealand Gazette and Wellington Spectator*, 5 September 1840.

21. *New Zealand Chronicle*, 11 November 1848; *Evening Post*, 27 May 1871.

22. *Evening Post*, 18 July 1883; *Nelson Evening Mail*, 1 March 1880; *Timaru Herald*, 4 June 1881; *Otago Witness*, 19 May 1892.

23. J.G. Findlay, *Anarchism: Its Origin and Aim – a lecture delivered in Wellington by J G Findlay, LLD*, Evening Star Job Printing Works, 1894.

24. Richard Hill, *The Iron Hand in the Velvet Glove: The Modernisation of Policing in New Zealand 1886–1917*, Dunmore Publishing, 1996, p. 353, p. 126, p125.

25. "Report by Henry Parker, Surveyor, and J. Lockie, and signed by Andrew McDonnell, Constable No. 782," BBAO-5544-69/A-1901/327, Archives New Zealand (ANZ).

26. Hermia Oliver, *The International Anarchist Movement in Late Victorian London*, Croom Helm, 1983, p. 13, p. 16.

27. Schmidt & van der Walt, *Black Flame*, p.123; Berry, *A History of the French Anarchist Movement*, p.21.

28. Barry Pateman, email to the author, 7 February 2012.

29. *NZ Times*, 16 September 1901.

30. It should be noted however that many anarchists still believed a period of revolutionary upheaval would include collective violence of some kind: "revolution must of necessity be violent, even though violence is in itself an evil. It must be violent because a transitional, revolutionary violence is the only way to put an end to the far greater, and permanent, violence which keeps the majority of mankind in servitude." Errico Malatesta. *Umanità Nova*, 12 August, 1920.

31. *NZ Times*, exact date unknown, 1901. Although outside of the broad anarchist tradition, Tolstoy's Christian anarchism had at least one prominent New Zealand follower, Harold Williams (1876–1928). Born in Auckland, Williams went on to become one of the world's most accomplished linguists, and considered by one historian as the most brilliant foreign correspondent his generation had ever known. Williams' knowledge of over fifty-eight languages saw him travel to Russia

to meet Tolstoy personally, write extensively on Russian affairs, and helped him become the Foreign Editor of *The Times* (UK) from 1922 untill his untimely death in 1928. Like Tolstoy, he was a vegetarian and believed in passive resistance.

32. *NZ Times*, September 1901; Valerie Smith, "'Gospel of Hope' or 'Gospel of Plunder': Socialism from the mid-1890s up to and including the Blackball Strike of 1908," BA Hons Research Essay, Massey University, 1976.

33. Taylor, "Workers' Vanguard or People's Voice?," p. 24.

34. Prebble, *"Troublemakers,"* p. 10–11. The current-day suburb of Wainoni, Christchurch is named in memory of Bickerton's home and includes Bickerton Street, Bickerton Reserve and Bickerton Tavern. A biography of Bickerton can be found here: http://www.teara.govt.nz/en/biographies/2b23/1

35. "Bert Roth to C. Demeulenaere," Biographical Notes-Foreigners, Bert Roth Collection, MS-Papers-6164-124, Alexander Turnbull Library (ATL), Wellington.

36. *NZ Times*, September 1901.

37. Ibid., exact date unknown, 1901.

38. Mark Derby, "Mahuki of the Red Plume—the intersection of labour and race politics in 1890," paper delivered at Globalisation and Labour in the Pacific: Re-evaluating the 1890 Maritime Strike, Auckland University of Technology, 4 November 2010.

39. Ibid.; Prebble, *"Troublemakers".*

40. Reason and Revolt, "Active Service Brigade," available online at http://www.reasoninrevolt.net.au/biogs/E000047b.htm.

41. Bob James, *Anarchism and State Violence in Sydney and Melbourne 1886–1896: An argument about Australian labor history*, available online at http://www.takver.com/history/aasv/index.htm. For example, Dr Thomas Fauset Macdonald did visit New Zealand after spending time in Australia (see Chapter 4).

4. WELLINGTON'S WORKING-CLASS COUNTER-CULTURE

1. *Cyclopedia of New Zealand*, as cited by David McGill, *Wellington: A Capital Century*, Transpress, 2003, p. 7.

2. Adrian Humphries and Geoff Mew, *Ring Around the City: Wellington's New Suburbs 1900–1930*, Steele Roberts, 2009, pp. 16–24.

3. "Naturalisation – Application for- Josephs, Philip," IA-1-20/1/1850, ANZ, Wellington.

4. *Wanganui Chronicle*, 15 March 1904.

5. Ibid.

6. "Chlieb I Volta!" (Freedom and Bread!), *Evening Post*, 29 January 1905.

7. *Evening Post*, 20 February 1905. Josephs was obviously comfortable writing and speaking in English before his arrival in Wellington.

8. Quail, *The Slow Burning Fuse*, p. 244.

9. Fran Shor, "Bringing the Storm: Syndicalist Counterpublics and the Industrial Workers of the World in New Zealand, 1908–14," in Pat Moloney & Kerry Taylor (eds), *On the Left: Essays on Socialism in New Zealand*, Dunedin, 2002, p. 60.

10. According to Bert Roth, Josephs joined the NZSP in 1906, although it is possible he joined in 1905 due to his role as a speaker at NZSP demonstrations. Either way, it is clear Olssen's claim that nothing in the history of the NZSP had forshadowed the 'new spirit' of the 1907–8 period is imprecise. For more information on the

NZSP, see Kerry Taylor, "Workers Vanguard or People's Voice?," and Bert Roth, "The New Zealand Socialist Party," *Political Science*, March 1957.

11. *Manawatu Standard*, 2 November 1900.

12. *Press*, 2 November 1900.

13. *Commonweal*, September 1907.

14. *NZ Truth*, 21 July 1906.

15. *Maoriland Worker*, 25 October 1912.

16. *Evening Post*, 30 June 1906.

17. Ibid., 2 July 1906.

18. Schmidt & van der Walt, *Black Flame*, p. 48.

19. Libcom, "Anarchist Communism—an Introduction," available online at http://libcom.org/thought/anarchist-communism-an-introduction.

20. *Maoriland Worker*, 10 May 1912.

21. Peter Kropotkin, *Words of a Rebel*, available online at http://dwardmac.pitzer.edu/anarchist_archives/kropotkin/words/wordsofarebeltoc.html; Schimdt and van der Walt, *Black Flame*, p. 71.

22. "Macdonald, Thomas Fauset, 1862–1910," Biographical Notes-Foreigners, Bert Roth Collection, MS-Papers-6164-123, ATL, Wellington; Oliver, *The International Anarchist Movement in Late Victorian London*, p. 93.

23. David Nicoll, *The Greenwich Mystery! A Commonweal pamphlet*, David Nicoll,1897, as cited by David Mulry, "Popular Accounts of the Greenwich Bombing and Conrad's *The Secret Agent*," accessed 4 April 2012 from http://rmmla.wsu.edu/ereview/54.2/articles/mulry.asp. It was this knowledge of chemical combustion that led Nicoll to imply Macdonald's connection to the Greenwich Bomb Incident of 1894 (when an anarchist named Martial Bourdin died after a bomb he was carrying exploded prematurely). Chemicals were supposedly 'stolen' from the doctor's surgery by an anarchist named Henry Benjamin Samuels (the brother-in-law of Bourdin), yet Samuels and Macdonald remained on good terms—the latter going so far as enthusiastically supporting Samuels during a *Commonweal* editorial dispute with Nicoll. In turn, Nicoll believed Macdonald was knowingly supplying Samuels, and even suggested the two were on the police payroll as agents provocateurs—although Nicoll's mental health, the bad blood between Nicoll and Samuels, and Macdonald's respected position in anarchist circles, makes the latter claim doubtful (for example, both Kropotkin and Nettlau defended Macdonald in the pages of *Freedom*). Nonetheless, it was enough to spur the pen of novelist Joseph Conrad into action. According to David Mulry, the character of Professor in Conrad's seminal work *The Secret Agent* is loosely based on Macdonald. However, this is disputed by Avrich, who believes an American anarchist named Professor Mezzerof was Conrad's true source. See "Conrad's Anarchist Professor: An Undiscovered Source," *Labour History*, 18(3), 1977.

24. *Commonweal*, July 1907.

25. Ibid., April 1907; June 1907; May 1907.

26. *Evening Post*, 13 June 1907.

27. *NZ Truth*, 6 July 1907; "MacDonald, Thomas Fauset, 1862–1910," Biographical Notes-Foreigners, Bert Roth Collection, MS-Papers-6164-123, ATL, Wellington.

28. "Dr. Thomas Fauset Macdonald to Max Nettlau," Nettlau Collection, International

Institute of Social History (IISH), Amsterdam.

29. *Commonweal*, July 1907.

30. *Nelson Evening Mail*, 1 November 1907.

31. *Evening Post*, 7 May 1906.

32. *Commonweal*, December 1906, as cited by Mark Derby, "Fuel of the Future: New Zealand Reactions to the Haymarket Martyrs," available online at http://redruffians.tumblr.com/post/2616619542/fuel-of-the-future-new-zealand-reactions-to-the.

33. *NZ Times*, 12 November 1907. Eagle would go on to become treasurer of the Wellington IWW and lecture on industrial unionism, despite the fact he was a "champion hall emptier" (Biographical Notes, Bert Roth Collection, MS-Papers-6164-024, ATL, Wellington). Even though Josephs is not mentioned by the *NZ Times*, he surely would have attended.

34. Derby, "Fuel of the Future."

35. Ibid.

36. *Evening Post*, 12 November 1907; *NZ Free Lance*, 16 November 1907.

37. Sutch, *The Quest for Security in New Zealand*, p. 102.

38. Taylor, "Workers Vanguard or People's Voice?," p. 40.

39. *Auckland Star*, 15 July 1911.

40. "T. Barker to B. Roth," Biographical Notes, Bert Roth Collection, MS-Papers-6164-007, ATL, Wellington.

41. *Evening Post*, 3 October 1908.

42. *Commonweal*, April 1907; *NZ Times*, exact date unknown, 1908.

43. "Account books," Freedom Collection, IISH, Amsterdam.

44. Jay Fox, "Trade Unionism and Anarchism (A Letter to a Brother Unionist)," available online at http://libertarian-labyrinth.org/archive/Trade_Unionism_and_Anarchism.

45. *Journal of the Department of Labour*, No.179, Vol.XVI, January 1908.

46. *Evening Post*, 26 August 1908.

47. Ibid., 29 March 1909.

48. Ibid.

5. TO HELL WITH LAW AND AUTHORITY

1. This chapter deals with the contentious relationship between anarchism, revolutionary syndicalism, and the IWW; its New Zealand manifestation would fill a book in itself. I have tried to approach this relationship using a framework discussed by Marcel van der Linden, where the subject is considered at an ideological, organizational, and shopfloor level (*Transnational Labour History: Explorations*, p. 74–75.) For the standards on this period see Eric Olssen, *The Red Feds: Revolutionary Industrial Unionism and the New Zealand Federation of Labor 1908–1913*, Oxford University Press, 1988; Melanie Nolan (ed.), *Revolution: The 1913 Great Strike in New Zealand*, Canterbury University Press, 2005; or more recently, Moriarty-Patten, "A World to Win".

2. Olssen, as cited by Michael King, *The Penguin History of New Zealand*, Penguin, 2003, p. 308.

3. Sutch, *The Quest for Security in New Zealand*, p. 100.

4. Roth, *Trade Unions in New Zealand*, p. 24.

5. *Ashburton Guardian*, 29 April 1910.

6. Roth & Hammond, *Toil and Trouble*, p. 70. There was illegal industrial action earlier that year, when in March 1906, fifty women in the Dunedin Tailoresses' Union were locked out in a dispute over preferential treatment. However, in this case the illegal action was taken by the employers. See Maryan Street, *The Scarlet Runners: Women and Industrial Action 1889–1913*, Working Life Communications, 1993, pp. 49–50.

7. Stanley Roche, *The Red and the Gold: An Informal Account of the Waihi Strike, 1912*, Oxford University Press, 1982. pp. 39, 40.

8. Roth, *Trade Unions in New Zealand*, p. 33.

9. Moriarty-Patten, "A World to Win," p. 15.

10. Roth, *Trade Unions in New Zealand*, p. 171; Moriarty-Patten, "A World to Win," p. 10.

11. *Commonweal*, January 1907.

12. *Grey River Argus*, 31 October 1907.

13. *Commonweal*, August 1907; July 1907.

14. "12 June 1908," McCullough Diary vol 1, McCullough papers, Canterbury Museum Library, Christchurch.

15. *Marlborough Express*, 25 July 1908.

16. Candace Falk, Barry Pateman & Jessica Moran (eds.), *Emma Goldman: A Documentary History of the American Years, Vol.1: Made for America, 1890–1901*, University of Illinois Press, 2008, p. 383; Oliver, *The International Anarchist Movement in Late Victorian London*, p. 48.

17. "20 February 1909," McCullough Diary vol 1, McCullough papers, Canterbury Museum Library, Christchurch; Prebble, *"Troublemakers,"* p. 3.

18. R Bailey, "Anarcho-Syndicalism in the N.Z. Labour Movement," in *NZ Labour Review*, May 1950, p. 27.

19. *Social Democrat*, 15 March 1912; 5 April 1912.

20. Ibid., 29 March 1912.

21. *Maoriland Worker*, 17 May 1912.

22. Ibid., 14 June 1911.

23. *Poverty Bay Herald*, 3 July 1911; *Ashburton Guardian*, 11 September 1911.

24. *Maoriland Worker*, 11 October 1912.

25. R Bailey, "Anarcho-Syndicalism in the NZ Labour Movement," p. 26.

26. *Social Democrat*, 15 March 1912.

27. *Weekly Herald*, 28 January 1911.

28. *Social Democrat*, January 26, 1912.

29. Ibid.

30. Ibid.

31. Ibid.

32. Ibid.

33. *Commonweal*, May 1907; June 1908; February 1908.

34. Ibid., July 1907; *Star*, 15 November 1907.

35. *Social Democrat*, 9 February 1912.

36. Ibid., 26 January 1912.

37. *Maoriland Worker*, 12 September 1913.

38. Ibid., 30 May 1913.

39. Ibid., 2 May 1913.

40. Morriaty-Patten, "A World to Win," p. 60.
41. Olssen, *The Red Feds*, p. 132.
42. Ibid., p. 129.
43. *Direct Action*, 27 November 1915, as cited by Moriarty-Patten, "A World to Win," p. 81.
44. Schmidt & van der Walt, *Black Flame*, pp. 159–160.
45. Olssen, *The Red Feds*, p. 132.
46. *Industrial Unionist*, 1 August 1913.
47. Ibid.
48. *Industrial Unionist*, 18 November 1913.
49. Moriarty-Patten, "A World to Win," pp. 44–46.
50. Ibid.
51. *Industrial Unionist*, 1 March 1913.
52. Ibid.
53. *Evening Post*, 4 December 1913.
54. *Thames Star*, 10 August 1912.
55. *Evening Post*, 4 February 1914.
56. *Evening Post*, 18 July 1914.
57. Olssen, *The Red Feds*, p. 132.
58. Ibid., p. 116; Eric Olssen, email to the author, 23 August 2010.
59. "A. Holdsworth to B. Roth," Biographical Notes-Foreigners, Bert Roth Collection, MS-Papers-6164-120, ATL, Wellington.
60. *Industrial Unionist*, 1 February 1913.

6. AN AGENT OF FREEDOM

1. "P. Josephs to T. Keel," 8 May 1911, Freedom Collection, IISH, Amsterdam.
2. "Philip Josephs of Johnsonville Manufacturing Clothier," Bankruptcies Register 1896–1910, AAOM-6048-6/, ANZ, Wellington.
3. "P. Josephs to T. Keel," 8 May 1911, Freedom Collection, IISH, Amsterdam.
4. *Commonweal*, January 1907.
5. *Evening Post*, 24 May 1913; *Commonweal*, March & April, 1909; J. Edgar Hoover.
6. *Social Democrat*, 28 July 1911.
7. *Maoriland Worker*, 4 August 1911.
8. Ibid., 4 July 1913.
9. Ibid., 4 July 1913; 4 August 1911.
10. Ibid., April 11, 1913.
11. Ibid., 10 November 1911; 13 July 1913.
12. Ibid., 13 December 1912; 11 April 1913.
13. Ibid., April 11, 1913.
14. Ibid., 1 April 1914.
15. Ibid., 10 November 1911.
16. Ibid., 11 April 1913.
17. "P. Josephs to T. Keel," 30 August 1911, Freedom Collection, IISH, Amsterdam.
18. *Maoriland Worker*, 10 November 1911.
19. Ibid., 26 January 1912.
20. "P. Josephs to T. Keel," 30 August 1911, Freedom Collection, IISH, Amsterdam.
21. *Freedom*, September 1912.

22. Ibid.
23. *Maoriland Worker*, 10 May 1912.
24. Ibid.
25. Ibid., 12 July 1912; *Freedom*, September 1912.
26. "P. Josephs to T. Keel," 30 August 1911, Freedom Collection, IISH, Amsterdam.
27. Ibid.; *Maoriland Worker*, 5 July 1912.
28. "Freedom Accounts Book," Freedom Collection, IISH, Amsterdam.
29. *Maoriland Worker*, 8 October 1912.
30. Ibid., 1 September 1911.
31. "P. Josephs to T. Keel," 26 May 1911, Freedom Collection, IISH, Amsterdam.
32. "P. Josephs to M. Nettlau," 1911, Nettlau Collection, IISH, Amsterdam.
33. Prebble, *"Troublemakers,"* p. 3. Nettlau's page on New Zealand mainly covers various articles on the labour movement and mentions the Waihi Strike of 1912. See http://redruffians.tumblr.com.
34. *Freedom*, September 1912.
35. J A Lee, *Simple on a Soapbox*, Auckland, 1963, p. 22, as cited in Moriarty-Patten, "A World To Win," p. 11.
36. Tom Mann, *Tom Mann's Memoirs*, Labour Publishing Company, 1923, p. 224; Cornelissen, as cited by Constance Bantman, "Internationalism without an International? Cross-Channel Anarchist Networks, 1880–1914," in *Labour International*, 84(4), 2006, p. 978.
37. Bantman, "Internationalism without an International?" p. 978.
38. *Mother Earth*, 1(8) October 1906; 5(7), July 1912.; 4(6), June 1911.
39. Ibid., 7(12) February 1913.
40. *Freedom*, January 1913; Oliver, *The International Anarchist Movement in Late Victorian London*, p. 78.
41. *The Spur*, October 1915; May 1920.
42. "A Conversation with a Syndicalist from New Zealand," c.1914, Nettlau Collection, IISH, Amsterdam.
43. Ibid.
44. Ibid.
45. Mark Derby, "Lola Ridge: anarchist and poet," available online at http://redruffians.tumblr.com/post/2617286625/lola-ridge-anarchist-and-poet.
46. Ibid.
47. Its secretary was a prominent figure in the labour and unemployed movement, Jim Edwards, who was radicalized by the case. Other members included Sid Scott, co-founder of the Auckland branch of the Communist Party of New Zealand. "Further conversations with New Zealand Ex-Communists," Campaign Against Foreign Control of Aotearoa Archives, Christchurch.
48. Ibid.

7. NO WAR BUT CLASS WAR

1. R.L. Weitzel, "Pacifists and Anti-militarists, 1909–1914," *New Zealand Journal of History*, 1973, p. 128.
2. Ryan Bodman, "'Don't Be a Conscript, Be a Man!' A History of the Passive Resisters' Union, 1912–1914," Thesis, University of Auckland, 2010, p. 8.
3. Ibid.

4. *Maoriland Worker*, 18 August 1911.
5. Ibid.
6. Ibid.
7. Ibid.
8. *Maoriland Worker*, April 12 1912; *Evening Post*, 2 May 1912; *Maoriland Worker*, April 19, 1912.
9. "P. Josephs to C. Mackie," 29 July 1912, Biographical Notes, Bert Roth Collection, MS-Papers-6164-045, ATL, Wellington.
10. "P. Josephs to C. Mackie," 6 December 1912, Biographical Notes, Bert Roth Collection, MS-Papers-6164-045, ATL, Wellington.
11. Bodman, "Don't Be a Conscript, Be a Man!" p. 2.
12. "P. Josephs to C. Mackie," 19 May 1913, Biographical Notes, Bert Roth Collection, MS-Papers-6164-045, ATL, Wellington.
13. *Maoriland Worker*, 18 August 1911.
14. *Evening Post*, 8 July 1913.
15. Ibid., 15 January 1915.
16. *Industrial Unionist*, 1 October 1913.
17. Allen, as cited by Weitzel, "Pacifists and Anti-militarists, 1909–1914," pp. 145–146.
18. "P. Josephs to C. Mackie," 19 May 1913, Biographical Notes, Bert Roth Collection, MS-Papers-6164-045, ATL, Wellington.
19. *Maoriland Worker*, 13 July 1913.
20. Ibid., 18 July 1913.
21. Ibid., 1 August 1913; 8 August 1913; 29 August 1913; *Evening Post*, 17 October 1913.
22. *Evening Post*, 9 October 1913; *Maoriland Worker*, 8 August 1913.
23. *Evening Post*, 13 February 1897; Biographical Notes, Bert Roth Collection, MS-Papers-6164-068, ATL, Wellington.
24. *Evening Post*, 12 February 1913; "Freedom Accounts Book," Freedom Collection, IISH, Amsterdam.
25. *Maoriland Worker*, 8 August 1913.
26. "New Zealand Socialist Party Minute Book," 12 September 1913, Gerald Griffin Collection, 86-043-2/18, ATL, Wellington.
27. *Maoriland Worker*, 3 October 1913.
28. Ibid., 15 October 1913.
29. Ibid.
30. *Industrial Unionist*, 1 October 1913.
31. Roth, *Trade Unionism in New Zealand*, p. 37.
32. Moriarty-Patten, "A World to Win," p. 23. For a succinct overview of the 1913 Great Strike, see Chapter 20 of Hill's *The Iron Hand in the Velvet Glove*.
33. *NZ Truth*, 8 November 1913, as cited by Moriarty-Patten, "A World To Win," p. 52.
34. Donald Anderson, "Crime as Protest in the Great Strike in Wellington," in Nolan (ed.), *Revolution*, p. 112.; Olssen, *The Red Feds*, p. 182.
35. Ibid.
36. Mark Derby, *The Prophet and the Policeman: The Story of Rua Kenana and John Cullen*, Craig Cotton Publishing, 2009, p. 54.
37. Hill, *The Iron Hand in the Velvet Glove*, p. 312.
38. Ibid.
39. Pat Lawlor, *Confessions of a Journalist*, Whitcombe & Tombs, 1913, pp. 20–21.

40. Peter Franks, "Chronology of events," in Nolan (ed.), *Revolution*, p. 14. Some specials clearly cherished the chance of cracking skulls. One baton, gifted to the Museum of New Zealand Te Papa Tongarewa in 2005, had the words 'Society combats anarchy brutality syndicalists' carefully engraved into it by its owner, Hugh White (GH011601).

41. 'The Waterfront Strike, 1913', from *An Encyclopaedia of New Zealand*, edited by A. H. McLintock, originally published in 1966. Te Ara - the Encyclopedia of New Zealand, available online at http://www.teara.govt.nz/en/1966/riots/5; NZ Truth, 29 November 1913.

42. *Evening Post*, 5 December 1913.

43. See Moriarty-Patten, "A World to Win," and Hill, T*he Iron Hand in the Velvet Glove*, p. 312; Derby, *The Prophet and the Policeman*, p. 54.

44. Prebble, *"Troublemakers,"* p. 18; Len Richardson, *Coal, Class and Community: The United Mineworkers of New Zealand 1880–1960*, Auckland University Press, 1995, p. 150.

45. "Police Report," 30 September 1915, Censorship of correspondence, P. Joseph to Miss E. Goldman, July–November, AAYS-8647-AD10-10/-19/16, ANZ, Wellington.

46. *Maoriland Worker*, 17 December 1913.

47. *Evening Post*, 12 November 1913.

8. PARASITES, ANARCHISTS, AND OTHER IWW TYPES

1. Moriarty-Patten, "A World to Win," p. 26.

2. New Zealand Employers Federation, *Organising and Defence Fund Schemes: a plea for the complete industrial organization of all employers of labour in New Zealand*, 1912, ATL; Moriarty-Patten, "A World to Win," pp. 26–27.

3. Moriarty-Patten, "A World to Win," p. 27.

4. J.A. Lee, *Simple on a Soapbox*, p. 23.

5. Shor, "Bringing the Storm," p. 71.

6. When discussing the possibility of conscripting men into the war effort, Defence Minister Allen noted: "We are right for it, and it is only the fear of what might happen in Labour circles that prevents it being adopted here." See Paul Baker, *King and Country Call: New Zealanders, Conscription and the Great War*, Auckland University Press, 1988, p.43, for other evidence to this end.

7. Alex Frame, *Salmond: Southern Jurist*, Victoria University Press, 1995, pp. 166–167.

8. John Anderson, "Military Censorship in World War 1: Its Use and Abuse in New Zealand," Thesis, Victoria University College, 1952, p. 246.

9. David Grant, *Field Punishment No. 1: Archibald Baxter, Mark Briggs & New Zealand's anti-militarist tradition*, Steele Roberts Publishers, 2008, p. 36.

10. Baker, *King and Country Call*, p. 168.

11. "Police Report," 12 April 1916, Menzel, R.O., Mumme, C., AAAB-449-5/I-29/147, ANZ, Wellington.

12. Lorna Wuthrich, "Carl Hinrich Andreas Mumme," available online at http://freepages.genealogy.rootsweb.ancestry.com/~chousmith/hinrich.htm; Lorna Wuthrich, email to the author, 30 May 2012.

13. "C. Mumme to J. Allen," 29 August 1916, Mumme, Karl, AAAB-482-24/o-234, ANZ, Wellington.

14. McGill, *Island Secrets*, p. 51.
15. "Carl Mumme to Major Matheson," 22 August 1916; 'Carl Mumme to Margaret Mumme,' 8 June 1916, Menzel, R.O., Mumme, C., AAAB-449-5/I-29/147, ANZ, Wellington.
16. "Report of Commandant, Somes Island," 6 February 1918, Mumme, Karl, AAAB-482-24/o-234, ANZ, Wellington.
17. "Re Prisoner of War No, S.I. 394. Karl Mumme," 18 August 1916, Menzel, R.O., Mumme, C., AAAB-449-5/I-29/147, ANZ, Wellington.
18. "Complaints from prisoners of war at Somes Island," 21 January 1918, Menzel, R.O., Mumme, C., AAAB-449-5/I-29/147, ANZ, Wellington.
19. Lorna Wuthrich, email to the author, 30 May 2012.
20. "Case of C.H.A.Mumme," 23 June 1916, Menzel, R.O., Mumme, C., AAAB-449-5/I-29/147, ANZ, Wellington.
21. "Police Report," 2 December 1918, Mumme, Karl, AAAB-482-24/o-234, ANZ, Wellington.
22. In 1921, Mumme found himself back in court on charges of not handing over his naturalization papers. Mumme told the magistrate the papers had been lost during his stint on Somes, cleared out by his son and probably burnt. Despite police pressure and repeated interviews, the magistrate gave Mumme the benefit of the doubt and he was not charged. In fact, Mumme had hidden the papers by inserting them into the interior of a large cabinet, found years later by his grand daughter after the cabinet had made its way to family in Australia.
23. *Evening Post*, 19 January 1917; 20 October 1917.
24. *Maoriland Worker*, 24 January 1917.
25. *Evening Post*, 16 January 1917.
26. *AJHR*, 1915, F1, p. 4.
27. Baker, *King and Country Call*, p. 78.
28. "Police Report," 30 September 1915, Censorship of correspondence, P. Joseph to Miss E. Goldman, July–November, AAYS-8647-AD10-10/-19/16, ANZ, Wellington.
29. *Direct Action*, 23 October 1915.
30. "Police Report," 12 October 1915, Censorship of correspondence, P. Joseph to Miss E. Goldman, July–November, AAYS-8647-AD10-10/-19/16, ANZ, Wellington.
31. Ibid.
32. Ibid.; *Direct Action*, 15 February 1915.
33. "P. Josephs to T. Keel," 30 August 1911, Freedom Collection, IISH, Amsterdam.
34. 'Anarchist Literature. Case of Philip Josephs," Salmond to the Comissioner of Police, Censorship of correspondence, P. Joseph to Miss E. Goldman, July–November, AAYS-8647-AD10-10/-19/16, ANZ, Wellington.
35. Ibid.
36. Ibid.
37. "Police Memorandum," 21 October 1915, Censorship of correspondence, P. Joseph to Miss E. Goldman, July–November, AAYS-8647-AD10-10/-19/16, ANZ, Wellington.
38. "Police Report," 28 October 1915; "Defence Department Memorandum," 28 October 1915, Censorship of correspondence, P. Joseph to Miss E. Goldman, July–November, AAYS-8647-AD10-10/-19/16, ANZ, Wellington.
39. "Freedom Accounts Book," Freedom Collection, IISH, Amsterdam.
40. *Maoriland Worker*, 11 June 1911.

41. "J. Sweeny to P. Josephs," 3 November 1915; "W.A. Tanner to Colonel Gibbon," 4 November 1915, Censorship of correspondence, P. Joseph to Miss E. Goldman, July–November, AAYS-8647-AD10-10/-19/16, ANZ, Wellington.

9. LOOSE ENDS

1. *NZ Truth*, 14 April 1917.
2. Ibid., 28 April 1917.
3. Ibid., 19 July 1919.
4. Ibid., 2 October 1920.
5. Ibid., 30 July 1921.
6. *Maoriland Worker*, 1 September 1920; last advert: 17 August 1921.
7. Lazarus Morris Goldman, *The History of the Jews in New Zealand*, Reed Publishing, 1958, p. 221.
8. *Freedom*, exact date unknown, 1920.
9. Ibid. Despite this letter's claims to the contrary, there was a considerable rise in class struggle in New Zealand in the 1917–1920 period. See Toby Boraman, "'The Aftermath of the 1912 Waihi Strike and the Second Wave of Syndicalism," conference paper, Waihi Centennial, 2012.
10. After the Freedom Group, the next specifically anarchist collectives in New Zealand formed in the early 60s. To pick up the anarchist story where this book ends, see Toby Boraman, *Rabble Rousers and Merry Pranksters: A History of Anarchism in Aotearoa/New Zealand from the Mid–1950s to the Early 1980s*, Katipo Books, 2007.
11. Wobblies Len Gale, Lew Williams, and Bob Edwards were involved in an underground press that carried on the artistic agitation and traditions of the IWW, including the famous depiction of FOL leader Fintan Patrick 'the Rat' Walsh. See *Clandestine! Illegal leaflets 1951*, elag, 2011.

EPILOGUE

1. Tobias, *The Jewish Bund in Russia*, p. 7.
2. Moriarty-Patten, "A World to Win," p. 53; "Leo Woods to Bert Roth", 15 December 1960, Biographical Notes, Bert Roth Collection, MS-Papers-6164, ATL, Wellington.
3. *Social Democrat*, 22 March 1912.
4. "Primary sources [on women] were always a problem for me in my research. I had to go off newspaper reports mostly and some union minutes, but those never described anybody as anarchist." Maryan Street, email to author, 23 May 2012.
5. Quail, *The Slow Burning Fuse*, p. 244.
6. Salvatore Salerno, *Red November, Black November: Culture and Community in the Industrial Workers of the World*, State University of New York Press, 1989, p. 144.
7. Ibid., p. 26.
8. Olssen, *The Red Feds*, p. 86.
9. Formed in 1927, the FAI was a large and influential anarchist federation that included affinity groups spread across the Iberian Peninsula. It played a major role in the Spanish union movement, as well as the Spanish Revolution of 1936. See Stuart Christie, *We, the Anarchists! A Study of the Iberian Anarchist Federation (FAI) 1927–1937*, AK Press, 2008.

10. Kerry Taylor, "Cases of the Revolutionary Left and the Waterside Workers' Union," in Nolan (ed), *Revolution*, p. 203.

11. Ibid.

12. Ibid., pp. 203–204.

13. Olssen, *The Red Feds*, p. 219.

14. Shor, "Bringing the Storm," p. 71; *Evening Post*, 7 February 1919.

15. Moriarty-Patten, "A World to Win," p. 131; Taylor, "A Case for the Revolutionary Left," p. 204; Boraman, "The Aftermath of the 1912 Waihi Strike and the Second Wave of Syndicalism."

16. Jeremy Breecher, *Strike! The True History of Mass Insurrection in America from 1877 to the Present—as authentic revolutionary movements against the establishments of state, capital and trade unionism*, Straight Arrow Books, 1972, p. 319.

17. Nicholas Lampert, "Struggles at Haymarket: An Embattled History of Static Monuments and Public Interventions" in Josh MacPhee & Eric Ruin (eds.), *Realizing the Impossible: Art Against Authority*, AK Press, 2007, p. 255.

ILLUSTRATION SOURCES

1. The Gorrie Collection, Library of the University of Leicester, United Kingdom.

2. HX826 F494 A, J.C.Beaglehole Room, Victoria University of Wellington, New Zealand.

3. Caroline Josephs, personal collection.

4. Caroline Josephs, personal collection.

5. Creator Unknown. Ref: PAColl-8195. ATL, Wellington, New Zealand. http://natlib.govt.nz/records/23023072

6. Biographical Notes, Bert Roth Collection, MS-Papers-6164-024, ATL, Wellington.

7. *Commonweal*, Hocken Library, University of Otago, New Zealand.

8. J.E. Tullett: Photographs, including images of Tauherenikau, Trentham and Featherston Military Camps and Templars' Cricket Club. Ref: PAColl-4435-01. ATL, Wellington, New Zealand. http://natlib.govt.nz/records/23134527.

9. *New Zealand Free Lance*, 22 June 1907, ATL, Wellington, New Zealand.

10. Muir and Moodie (Firm). Photograph taken by Muir and Moodie. Roth, Herbert Otto, 1917–1994 :Photographs. Ref: 1/1-002591-F. ATL, Wellington, New Zealand. http://natlib.govt.nz/records/22304421

11. Lorna Wuthrich, personal collection.

12. Freedom Broadsheets Collection, Kate Sharpley Library.

13. *Maoriland Worker*, 10 May 1912, ATL, Wellington, New Zealand.

14. Freedom Collection, IISH, Amsterdam.

15. 7-A10659, Sir George Grey Special Collections, Auckland Libraries, New Zealand.

16. *New Zealand Observer*, 16 December 1916, ATL, Wellington, New Zealand.

17. "Censorship of correspondence, P Joseph to Miss E Goldman, July-November," Archives New Zealand/ Te Rua Mahara o te Kawanatanga, Wellington Office. [AD 10 box 10 19/16].

18. Ibid.

19. Ibid.

20. Ibid.

21. Helen Dukes, personal collection.

22. Caroline Josephs, personal collection.

Support AK Press!

AK Press is one of the world's largest and most productive

anarchist publishing houses. We're entirely worker-run and democratically managed. We operate without a corporate structure—no boss, no managers, no bullshit. We publish close to twenty books every year, and distribute thousands of other titles published by other like-minded independent presses from around the globe.

The Friends of AK program is a way that you can directly contribute to the continued existence of AK Press, and ensure that we're able to keep publishing great books just like this one! Friends pay a minimum of $25 per month, for a minimum three month period, into our publishing account. In return, Friends automatically receive (for the duration of their membership), as they appear, one free copy of every new AK Press title. They're also entitled to a 20% discount on everything featured in the AK Press Distribution catalog and on the website, on any and every order. You or your organization can even sponsor an entire book if you should so choose!

There's great stuff in the works—so sign up now to become a Friend of AK Press, and let the presses roll!

Won't you be our friend? Email friendsofak@akpress.org for more info, or visit the Friends of AK Press website: http://www.akpress.org/programs/friendsofak